# The Barefoot
# NAVIGATOR

## JACK LAGAN

**SHERIDAN HOUSE**

This edition published 2006 by
Sheridan House Inc.
145 Palisade Street
Dobbs Ferry, NY 10522
www.sheridanhouse.com

Library of Congress Cataloging-in-Publication Data

Lagan, Jack.
  The barefoot navigator / by Jack Lagan; illustrated by
  Jack Lagan.
      p. cm.
  Includes index.
  ISBN 1-57409-232-4 (pbk. : alk. paper)
1.  Navigation—Handbooks, manuals, etc. 2.  Boats and
boating—Handbooks, manuals, etc. 3.  Seamanship—
Handbooks, manuals, etc.  I. Title.

VK155.L34 2006
623.89'23—dc22
            2006003657

Note: While all reasonable care has been taken in the
production of this publication, the publisher takes no
responsibility for the use of the methods or products
described in the book.

ISBN  1-57409-232-4

Printed in Great Britain

# Contents

Printable versions of the graphics in the Appendices can be downloaded from:
www.jack-lagan.com

# Conventions and Credits

**DISTANCES** In general terms, distances are given in kilometres, except where a distance is given in statute miles within a quotation. In those cases, a metric equivalent is provided.

**MEASUREMENTS** Measurements generally are in metric, although I may occasionally slip into feet when giving the length overall of a boat.

**NAVIGATION DISTANCES** When discussing navigation at sea, distances are given in nautical miles (nm) for the simple reason that it is the only measure that derives from the geometry of the Earth. That's the way it has to be.

**DATES** Dates are quoted using the new convention. 'AD' is now 'CE' (Common Era) and 'BC' is 'BCE' (Before Common Era).

**TIME** Greenwich Mean Time (GMT) is now referred to as Universal Time or Universal Time Corrected (UT or UTC). But it is also sometimes referred to as 'World Time' and, by the military, as 'Zulu Time'. I quite like the sound of World Time, but will use UT and GMT in this book. Actual times are shown as four digits, without punctuation and always using the 24-hour clock.

**MAPS** Unless otherwise sourced, the maps were produced using Map Maker PRO. Available from: www.mapmaker.com.

**STAR CHARTS** Images of the night sky were created using Patrick Chevalley's *Cartes du Ciel* software. This is available from www.astrosurf.com/astropo.

**ASTROPHYSICS** Thanks to Keith Burnett, a college mathematics teacher and astronomy enthusiast, for his sound advice and disclaimer regarding the accuracy of everything on his useful website at: www.xylem.f2s.com/kepler/.

# A Barefoot Philosophy for the 21st Century

## GPS: THE DEATH OF NAVIGATION?

IF I HAD A NUGGET OF GOLD for every time I'd been told that the Global Positioning System (GPS) had spelled the demise of the shipboard navigator, I would be sailing an Oyster 72 *and* be able to afford the mooring fees. It is certainly true that a 'GPS user' is not the same thing as a wily wayfinder, especially one who doesn't throw up after ducking below in bad conditions but can conjure up a decent meal in indecent weather. In other words, there is a lot more to navigation than pushing a button to get a course to steer to the next waypoint.

This book is not a rant against modern technology. People of the contemporary world, especially the 21st-century seafarer, have every reason to admire satellite navigation as one of the most remarkable achievements of their own era. The efforts of the aerospace industry and microchip manufacturers intercept at the traffic lights and tell someone who has never seen the sea to turn left into the supermarket car park. Even I have one of those gadgets and I love it. But this book is about something else.

*The Barefoot Navigator* renews emphasis on personal skills, special knowledge and the use of the senses – especially the real sixth sense, common sense. I remember clearly the first time I saw this kind of thing in action; I was 19 and fishing for sharks in the English Channel on a Falmouth boat called *Huntress*. Shortly after first light we cast off from Custom House Quay and headed south out of Carrick Roads. After an hour or so we were somewhere off Rosemullion Head. This much I knew. But skipper Robin Vinnicombe was a Cornishman born and bred and these were his waters. I put *Huntress* into neutral and Robin stood by the fighting chair and peered through the mist, first west towards the Helford Estuary and then north back towards Pendennis Point. There were no charts or pilots on board; all that was in the skipper's head. He was trying to put us on a very precise point where we could haul the mizzen sail and drift to the east, leaving a trail of chum to tease in the Blues and, hopefully, the Holy Grail, that really big Mako. Finally Robin nodded; we were in the right place, we could bait the hooks.

Of course, Robin Vinnicombe didn't see anything special in what he was doing. Once I'd learned coastal navigation *I* could use a hand compass to take bearings on two or three marks, convert from magnetic to true, draw the position lines on the chart and, eventually, get a great fix. Robin's magic lay in knowing so many transits that he didn't need the compass and his cranial chart of that area off the Lizard Peninsula was so damned good that he didn't need any help from hydrographers either. Of course, I can use my coastal navigation skills anywhere on the planet, but I need a bearing compass and the right chart – or the local version of Robin Vinnicombe. The other consideration here is that we are looking at the very earliest form of navigation: coast-hugging. Once out of sight of land, different techniques come into play, methods that enabled ancient peoples to undertake long ocean voyages and that were the starting point for what I call 'barefoot navigation'.

Decades after my fishing expeditions off Falmouth, in the early days of GPS, I was planning a daylight passage on a 42ft sloop over an open stretch of water between two islands in the Caribbean. The distance was only about 60nm, but it was important to make landfall before dark. Once offshore, we encountered a heavy swell coming from astern. We quartered the sea to get a more comfortable ride but, as that was a couple of points off our steering course, I plotted a GPS fix every couple of hours, increasing the frequency as we got closer to our destination. What was making me edgy was the need to avoid getting caught off a lee shore before rounding the island and then having to find the anchorage on the far side behind a reef. It didn't turn out to be a problem; the sun touched the horizon as our CQR touched the bottom. What was interesting, though, was that our desire for a comfortable trip and paying attention to our angle to the swell also gave us a straight-line course for over 50 miles. A local boatman would have known that of course; one look at the direction of the swell would have determined his strategy for the crossing. That's barefoot navigation. Only my unfamiliarity with the area made me resort to technology for peace of mind.

This is small beer when compared with the skills deployed in the days of low-tech navigation. This is how the redoubtable Joshua Slocum describes his fog-bound approach to Ilha Grande off the coast of Brazil. It was April 1887 and he was captain of the merchant barque *Aquidneck* out of New York:

> Down the river and past the light-ship we came once more, this time with no halt to make, no backing sails to let a pilot off, nothing at all to stop us; we spread all sail to a favourable breeze, and reached Ilha Grande eight days afterward, beating the whole fleet by two days. Garfield kept strict account of this. He was on deck when we made the land, a dark and foggy night it was! Nothing could be seen but the dimmest outline of a headland through the haze. I knew the place, I thought, and Garfield said he could smell land, fog or coal-tar. This, it will be admitted, was reassuring. A school of merry porpoises that gamboled under the bows while we stood confidently in for the land, diving and crossing the bark's course in every direction, also guarded her from danger. I knew that so long as deepsea porpoises kept with us we had nothing to fear of the ground. When the lookout cried, 'Porpoises gone,' we turned the bark's head offshore, backed the

> maintops'l, and sent out the 'pigeon' [lead]. A few grains of sand and one soft, delicate white shell were brought up out of fourteen fathoms of water. We had but to heed these warnings and guides, and our course would be tolerably clear, dense and all as the fog and darkness was.
>
> The lead was kept constantly going as we sailed along in the intense darkness, till the headland of our port was visible through the haze of grey morning. What Garfield had smelled, I may mention, turned out to be coal-tar, a pot of which had been capsized on deck by the leadsman, in the night.[1]

Oh well, at least Garfield had all the makings of a barefoot navigator; and he was the ship's boy, not the ship's cat.

On passages measured in days rather than hours, other elements come into play. Are we still sheeted the same as yesterday for these Trade Winds? Is the sun still rising on our starboard quarter and setting just left of the bow? And then the overture to landfall; a white petrel arrives to fish and, as we watch it leave, we notice a wisp of cumulus above the horizon. Land? We make a slight adjustment to our course. Land!

## A STRATEGY FOR THE FUTURE

*'It is far better to have absolutely no idea of where one is
– and to know it – than to believe confidently
that one is where one is not.'*

Jean Dominique Cassini, *Astronomer*, 1770

As the passion for recreational offshore sailing grew in the second half of the 20th century, so did an awareness for the need to teach boat-handling skills and navigation on a more formal and standardised basis. At the forefront of this development was the Royal Yachting Association (RYA)[2]. For what must be 20 years, the RYA has developed and administered a carefully structured set of courses that meet the needs of everyone from children learning to sail dinghies to those wanting to venture across the high seas. Having (belatedly) taken some of these courses, I can vouch for their soundness and practicality; they have saved lives and helped thousands to enjoy their time at sea.

The navigational content of the RYA courses is best represented by two first-rate books. In the first, *The RYA Book of Navigation*[3], author Tim Bartlett covers all the ground (except weather and the Rules of the Road) up to Yachtmaster™ Offshore. This is just theory of course; you have to pass a shorebased course and then get through a practical assessment at sea to be awarded the ticket. Much of

1, 2, 3 et seq – *see* Notes page 125

the material is essential 'driving licence' stuff: charts, latitude and longitude, measuring distances and direction, lights and buoys and tides – an important consideration in British waters. Position fixing, estimating a course and passage planning are all done with the right emphasis on the fundamental concept of *vectors*, a good understanding of which is essential to all forms of navigation. And, for good measure, Bartlett adds chapters on the use of satellite navigation and radar.

*Ocean Yachtmaster*™ 4 takes over where the previous book leaves off. Apart from sections on global weather systems and passage planning, this is essentially a course in astro-navigation using a sextant. Now it's not just a question of getting across the Channel to France, but of safely reaching Tenerife for the transatlantic passage to Barbados. That first leg will in itself easily exceed the 600nm distance needed to get through the practical part of the Ocean Yachtmaster™ ticket – so long as you stay out of sight of France, Spain and Portugal and keep a detailed and accurate log of your work with the sextant. The assessment is done by interrogation; you have to convince a seasoned old RYA-appointed salt that you sailed as skipper or first mate and that really is your handwriting and calculation in the coffee-stained log. There is probably no better way of doing it and the RYA courses have been adopted around the world as far as Australia, South Africa and the Caribbean.

But this is where I have a problem. In the era of satellite navigation, it makes no particular sense to have your skills as an ocean navigator tested by your aptitude with a sextant. You might just as well use a quadrant, a backstaff or even an astrolabe for the purpose; they do the same job to differing degrees of accuracy and are equally obsolete in any role other than that of teaching fundamental concepts and as the regalia of the shaman of the sea. If you safely undertook your trial voyage from the Solent to the Azores with no instrumentation other than an emergency GPS set in a locked and sealed box, would that cause you to fail your Ocean Yachtmaster™ assessment? Yes, it would. The skills of the barefoot navigator are no better than those of the sextant-user, but they are different. I would also propose that barefoot knowledge cannot be put back in a casket in the same way that a sextant and navigation tables can. There must be more than a few ocean navigators who have done just that after passing their grilling by the examiner – they put the sextant back in its box (or on the mantelpiece) and switched on the GPS system.

I am not, as should now be evident, arguing that the venerable history of navigation be scuttled in favour of the pocket GPS set but, on the contrary, that it be embraced to enhance the fundamental wayfinding skills of all seafarers.

*The Barefoot Navigator*, then, is part history, part textbook and part polemic. It comprises four main parts.

Part 1 ('The Remarkable Skills of the Ancients') is an introduction to the basics of barefoot navigation written in the context of the strategies and techniques believed to have been used by wayfarers long before the advent of the most rudimentary technology. This will enable the reader to become acquainted with the fundamentals of navigating at sea without compass, charts, timepiece and sextant, while enjoying a few tales of exploration and adventure.

Part 2 ('Practical No-Tech Navigation') is more specifically concerned with the practical considerations of exploiting the same special knowledge used by the ancients; after all, the sun still rises in the east and sets in the west and will continue to do so for the foreseeable future. Not all these methods can be employed at all times of day; the stars cannot be seen during the day and, without being able to see the horizon, their elevation can't be measured. For this reason, the available techniques are grouped according to the time of day at which they are most appropriate: dawn, day, dusk and night. As a hardcore barefoot navigator you will be using the wind and the clouds, the ocean swells, marine wildlife and the sun; at night you will be using the stars.

If the Vikings could get a rough latitude by using a notched stick and the Pole Star, so can barefoot navigators – they just need to improvise a suitable stick. Part 3 of the book ('Do-It-Yourself Lo-Tech Navigation') contains a set of techniques for barefoot navigation in the 21st century. It includes everything the reader has discovered in the previous sections, with the addition of a few basic modern extras. These include a quartz watch (sadly indispensable if we are going to get a longitude), simple tables for reducing sun and star sights, a protractor, a poem, a ruler, a piece of string and the lid from a can of baked beans. An ancient navigator would have passed his star compass on to his son, so I don't see why you shouldn't have one – but you might have to make it yourself.

Finally, at the back of the book, are sections describing a navigator's survival kit, and a series of appendices that include the navigation tables as well as schematics for the assembly of DIY navigation instruments. So that you don't have to cut pages from the book, all the information and drawings in the appendices are included on my website at: http://jack-lagan.com.

So, my objective is this. When you finish this book and place it conveniently near the navigation table, you will be a better navigator than you were when you read this introduction. You will be able to boast new practical skills. These might only come into play in a survival situation or during an on-board party. However, with practice, you will be able to stand on deck, look at the sky and the sea around you and just kind of know where you are. You will be a barefoot navigator.

**JACK LAGAN**

**A CAUTIONARY NOTE**

This book has the objective of turning you into a barefoot navigator, but it is not part of my plan to turn you into a reckless navigator along the way. Do not go to sea without up-to-date charts, navigation tools and the training to use them. Compared with the use of GPS, barefoot techniques are approximate only, so be cautious and be conservative. If at all in doubt, do not put your boat and the lives of your crew at risk. Sail safe.

# PART ONE

# The Remarkable Skills of the Ancients

MOST SEA-FARING CULTURES probably made their own contributions to seamanship and navigation. Apportioning credit might be a risky undertaking but in this book I have concentrated on those peoples about whom we know most: the Pacific Islanders, the Vikings and the Arabs. I am sceptical about the Chinese, but they are included for reasons that will become clear.

The absence of writing and common languages made the transfer of knowledge within and across regional cultures difficult. So much of what was known in the South Pacific and elsewhere can only have been passed on by word-of-mouth; primarily by using the system of masters and apprentices for the practical stuff, poetry and song for the achievements of the great exponents. The Arabs were the first to write down sailing directions, as far as we know.

# The Pacific Islanders

*It is extraordinary that the same Nation should have spread themselves
all over the isles in this vast ocean from New Zealand to this Island
which is almost a fourth part of the circumference of the Globe.*

Captain James Cook, Easter Island, March 1774 [5]

## JUST ANOTHER DAY IN PARADISE?

THE OCEAN TRAVELLERS of the South Pacific, particularly the Polynesians, are the most impressive seafarers the world has ever seen. The epic migration that populated the Pacific started 4,000 years ago in South-East Asia, moving through what is now Indonesia, Melanesia and throughout Polynesia; as far north as Hawaii, as far east as Rapanui, as far south as New Zealand (see Fig 1.1).

Since the 1950s there has been controversy among academics about the eastern limit of this huge domain. Norwegian anthropologist Thor Heyerdahl[6] was so convinced that there had been a pattern of migration from *east to west* across the Pacific that he built a balsa wood raft and set out from South America to prove the point. It was a courageous undertaking, but linguistic patterns, archaeology and recent DNA research prove that Heyerdahl was wrong; Rapanui (Easter Island) was populated by Polynesians, not indigenous South Americans. Also, extensive radiocarbon dating in the region reveals no east to west migration trend.[7] Adventurous native Peruvians may well have made journeys of exploration to the west and they usually had wind and current in their favour. But a balsa raft and a sweet potato on a Tuamotu beach does not constitute a migration pattern.

To underscore the point about the navigation skills of the Polynesians, Rapanui was not just one more island below the horizon. It is some 1,200nm (about 2,000km) east of Pitcairn and Henderson Islands, if that is where the settlers departed from. Indeed, current thinking suggests that this distance may have been a contributory factor in the extinction of the island's population. In other words, the Polynesians overstretched themselves.

These movements of people across immense and uncharted stretches of open sea continued until as late as 1000 CE; they had settled just about all the inhabitable islands of the Pacific long before the Europeans turned up.

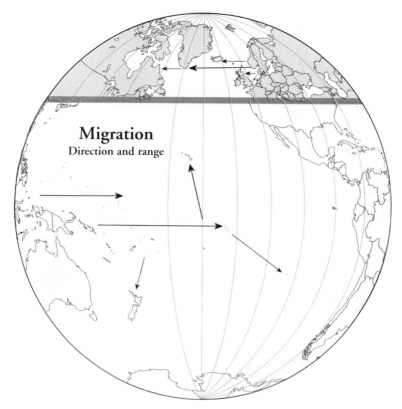

**Fig 1.1** Comparative patterns of migration in the North Atlantic and South Pacific.

It is unlikely in my opinion that this could have happened by chance or mishap, a view now taken by most modern archaeologists:

> …long-term experiments at ocean voyaging in replica canoes, using traditional navigational techniques, have provided indisputable proof that the settlement of the Pacific Islands was the result of deliberate voyaging, not accidental strandings far offshore.[8]

The Vikings were considerable navigators too, but the truth is they only had to miss Greenland to discover Vinland, what we now call North America. And that is precisely how it happened. Later in this section, we will consider the very special contributions made by Norse seafarers to practical navigation skills. But pride of place goes to the people of the pre-historical South Pacific:

> To understand the real achievements of the Polynesians one needs to lie on the hard, smelly deck of a wallowing copra ship for a week or so; this is about all the average landlubber without a yacht can do these days, and it is a salutary experience never to be forgotten.[9]

So speaks average landlubber and historian Peter Bellwood about the downside of one of his field trips to the region. He should be told that it's not much better on some yachts.

## *TANGATA*: THE GODS OF NAVIGATION

The lore of the Pacific says that the first great navigators were the original Polynesians, gods who called themselves *tangata*. Possessing magical powers, they could navigate by looking at the sea and sky and would never get lost. The oral tradition claims that these giants settled on the islands and married human women. Today's Polynesians are the fruit of these unions; and if you are descended from the gods, how can you fail? Describing the people who discovered your home islands as 'gods' is a way of showing respect – something like the reverence shown by Americans to Christopher Columbus and to the Pilgrim Fathers. But we don't need to look for mystical gods with supernatural powers to understand how the Polynesians learned to navigate without GPS receivers tied to their outriggers.

The driving force for the people of the Pacific was economic survival. As groups of families populated new islands, they would multiply and prosper until, over generations, they inevitably outgrew the natural resources of their new home. They would then scout out previously uninhabited islands even further to the east. If the reports of the pathfinders were favourable, they would load up their vessels and head out through the reef and turn in the direction of the rising sun.

It is mistaken to suggest that Polynesian migration sort of just happened, as though one day they would get bored with the atoll they had lived on for five generations and would set off to find a better paradise. Some sources claim that fleets of up to 100 boats would make these passages.[10] They knew the scale of the Pacific and understood its dangers far too well to risk putting out to sea with their children, livestock and other worldly possessions without knowing exactly where they were going and how long it would take. The implication is that they had 'pathfinders' who would not only seek out new islands but – and this is a crucial measure of successful navigation – *were able to find them again*. The fact that 'house moving' voyages rarely took much longer than 20 days[11] supports the idea of this strategy; that's easily 1,000nm (about 1,800km), manageable in terms of provisioning and well within the time usually taken for the onset of scurvy.

These flotillas of humanity owed their safety and their future to three things: the boatbuilding skills of their fishermen; their physical ability to survive ocean voyages; and the wayfaring capabilities of their navigators.

The audacious Polynesians did not have to make do with rafts. They were innovative boatbuilders able to produce small sailing canoes with single outriggers, twin-hulled *wakas* (the Polynesian 'sports utility vehicle') and even large multihulls – trimarans able to carry scores of passengers. These boats were mostly unstressed; without the technology to make rigid cross-members, the solution was to allow them to 'bend' with the waves. The result may have looked somewhat ramshackle but, if they had not been up to the job, the builders would have modified them. Fore-and-aft boomed sails, sometimes in a two-masted configuration, gave the vessels the ability to sail reasonably close to the wind. (A windward capability is something not possible with a raft unless it is being towed.)

At its peak, in the 10th century, the boatbuilding skills of the Pacific people were such that they could break the 'twenty day rule':

> The early Polynesians underwent hardships which few modern people could even visualize. The 4,000-kilometre voyage from the Society to the Hawaiian Islands may occupy only a few inches on a map, but in a partially open canoe laden with men, women, children, animals and precious seed plants it could easily have become an appalling ordeal. The astounding fact is that the Polynesians reached virtually every island within the huge Polynesian triangle, although by no means all were permanently settled.[12]

The 'Polynesian triangle' was more of a 'Polynesian polygon' (see Fig 1.2).

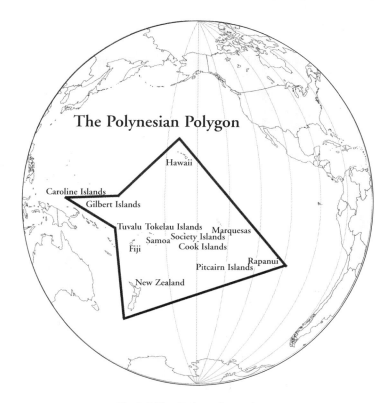

**Fig 1.2** The Polynesian polygon.

The key players in this grand survival strategy were the navigators. How did they manage to find their way across open seas without compass and sextant? And how did they pass that knowledge on from one generation to the next without a written language?

## 'FEELERS OF THE SEA'

As in most societies, knowledge was power. Essential travel and trade between the islands was totally dependent upon the wise men, the navigators, and the practical men, the skippers. In Tahiti, the *oripo* were bards who could recite the family trees of the navigators and captains who first discovered the islands. Descended from this group of pioneers was Nana-Ula who, in the 10th century CE, led a grand expedition of his people from Tahiti to Hawaii, a distance of some 2,100nm (about 4,000km). Nana-Ula later became the first King of Hawaii.

But what was the special knowledge that enabled the navigators to achieve these feats? How did they find their way across open seas without any form of technology as we know it? Samoan legend speaks of an old navigator called Kahomovailahi, or 'Kaho'. In spite of being totally blind, Kaho could determine the exact location of a boat merely by leaning over the side and touching the water. Kaho once guided the King of Samoa's boat to land, an achievement that so impressed the King he granted Kaho the equivalent of a knighthood. If the legendary Kaho was based on a real person, I suspect that the hand doing the navigating was really that of his apprentice. A simple coded tap on the old man's leg would have told him that the small cumulus cloud signposting the island was just off the port bow… notwithstanding this little bit of showmanship, Kaho's sons and grandsons carried on the navigator's traditions and they became known as *Fafaki-Tahi*, 'Feelers of the Sea'.

## THE CHART IN CAPTAIN WILLIAM BLIGH'S HEAD

The history of Polynesia is cluttered with boundless nonsense about the seafaring skills of the people of the Pacific. It is understandable that the ancients often sought out mystical explanations for gaps in their knowledge of the world around them; it is inexcusable for 21st century people (including some academics) to attribute mystical explanations for their achievements.

I have recently read that, 'The Polynesians relied upon astronomy to steer their canoes while sailing around the ocean… It was therefore necessary for this group of islanders to keep strict records of which stars rose where and when they were visible in the night sky.'[13] Without any writing technology it is hard to determine how such 'strict records' might have been kept. The same author goes on to state that, 'Using the "pits" along the horizon and the stars that passed through the zenith, the sailors were able to determine their latitude and longitude.' If that were indeed the case, John Harrison could have saved himself a lifetime of hard work building an accurate and reliable chronometer.

This could be written off as poor research, but some propositions are based on little more than New Age-style speculation:

> People can navigate across oceans and arrive at their destination by using their comfort zone. (Gut feelings, intuitive forces.) Where there is a lack of knowledge and the need to know, we base final decisions on intuitive forces. This is how we achieve any goal in life, whether it be sailing across oceans, building a business, or any achievement. Success depends on making right decisions where facts are missing. Comfort zone navigation is how the Polynesians populated the Pacific Ocean. Facts were extremely limited.[14]

So, if 'comfort zone navigation is how the Polynesians populated the Pacific Ocean', all we need to know now is: what is a 'comfort zone' and how can it be used.

Bob Webb, a motivational lecturer, is saying that the ocean is a no-comfort zone. An island hundreds of miles over the horizon is a comfort zone. If you sail off – in any direction to start with – you will unconsciously make course adjustments until you arrive at the island where you will be in a comfort zone and, therefore, very happy. This rather begs the question of why you left harbour in the first place; and why you didn't immediately circle back to it.

Navigation is a science, a craft and, arguably, an art; the suggestion that the accumulated knowledge of centuries of navigation can be discarded in favour of a 'touchy-feely' notion like this sets off my nonsense proximity alarm. Bob Webb's pitch for comfort zone navigation does not include references to any historical or scientific research, nor to any fieldwork in Polynesia. He does, however, cite the 1789 case of the 'Mutiny on the Bounty':

> The crew finally had enough, mutinied, and cast Captain Bligh and eighteen of his loyal crew members adrift in a lifeboat. Without navigation tools, they sailed the open boat 3,600 miles to the Dutch colony, Timor, near Java. This outstanding achievement is only possible with comfort zone navigation.[15]

I disagree. Although he had no chart, Bligh did have a quadrant, sight reduction tables and a chronometer – almost certainly a Harrison H4[16] or one of its early clones. He had been to that part of the Pacific before when he'd served on the *Resolution* as Captain James Cook's 22-year-old sailing master; his chart was in his head. This is what really happened:

> Once adrift, Bligh reverted to the master mariner and navigator that he was. Using the chronometer that [Fletcher] Christian had given him, Bligh had to navigate from memory over 62 days and some 3,600 miles of ocean, through the reefs of Fiji, the Great Barrier Reef and the Torres Strait and on to Timor. In memory of what remains one of the world's greatest open-boat journeys and feats of seamanship, several reefs in this region bear his name.[17]

After he'd returned to the Pacific to complete the breadfruit assignment he'd started in 1789, Bligh resumed his naval career and was commended by Admiral Nelson for his bravery in the Battles of Camperdown and Copenhagen. In 1801 he was elected a Fellow of the Royal Society for his services to navigation. As well as being grossly misinformed about this distinguished mariner, Mr Webb is being very patronising to the Polynesians. He may be right in suggesting that, when there is a shortage of 'facts' (or 'strict records'), gut feelings kick in. But although the Polynesians might have been short of written knowledge, that does not imply they were short of any kind of knowledge; they had a great oral tradition whereby navigators would pass the wisdom down from one generation to the next. They also had the considerable memories needed to achieve this and, like the much-maligned Captain William Bligh, could keep a chart in their heads.

## TUPAIA'S CHART

During the *Endeavour*'s 1769 visit to Tahiti, Captain James Cook's 'science officer', Sir Joseph Banks, took time out from befriending the local women to befriend their navigator-chief, a man called Tupaia (sometimes spelled 'Tupia'). Tupaia wanted to go to England, but the skipper was reluctant to take him. Banks, a wealthy man, convinced Cook by offering to sponsor Tupia and by pointing out that he was a navigator. This is Banks's journal entry for 12 July 1769 (original spelling kept throughout):

> 12. This morn Tupia came on board, he had renewd his resolves of going with us to England, a circumstance which gives me much satisfaction. He is certainly a most proper man, well born, cheif *Tahowa* or preist of this Island, consequently skilld in the mysteries of their religion; but what makes him more than any thing else desireable is his experience in the navigation of these people and knowledge of the Islands in these seas; he has told us the names of above 70, the most of which he has himself been at.[18]

Shown here in Fig 1.3 is the chart that one of Cook's officers sketched from Tupia's description of his cranial map.

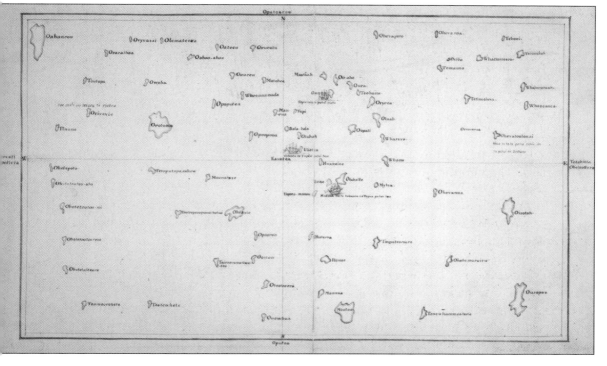

**Fig 1.3** Tupaia's chart of part of the South Pacific.[19]

It has been estimated that two-thirds of the islands are readily identifiable. The apparent errors can be attributed to translation problems rather than mistakes by Tupaia. For example, Cook assumed that, when Tupaia talked about an 'east' wind, he meant that it came from the *east* – the European convention – whereas he actually meant that it went *to* the east. (This strongly suggests that the chart in the Tahitian's head had a wind compass rose stamped on it.) The *Endeavour's* exotic new navigator was soon put to the test:

> Tupaia guided Cook 300 miles south to Rurutu, a small Polynesian island, proving he could navigate from his homeland to a distant island. Cook was amazed to find that Tupaia could always point in the exact direction in which Tahiti lay, without the use of the ship's charts.[20]

Tupaia had been to Rurutu before in his own sailing canoe. Interestingly, he told the British sailors that his father had told him that there were more islands even further to the south; that's how the oral tradition works in practice.

So, Tupaia didn't just know the names of more than 70 islands throughout Polynesia; he knew where they were and how to get to them. He also *proved* he had been to them by safely piloting *Endeavour* through the reef of each one they visited while giving Banks and the Captain a *Rough Guide* to the island's people, politics and economy. And not a comfort zone in sight.

# STRATEGIES AND TACTICS

Ancient seafarers navigated using what they could see around them: the ocean and the sky. Even with a little help from the marine wildlife, that would not seem to be enough to stake your life on. It could, however, be very accurate – but without the 24/7 consistency we expect from GPS. This obliged the navigators to change their techniques at different times of the day.

But what had to come first was a strategy for the voyage. This depended on the answer to the question: 'Have we been there before?' If the answer was 'No', the strategy would depend on knowledge of the prevailing winds or, in tropical regions, the Trade Winds. Even in a vessel with some windward capability, just setting off downwind could end up being a one-way trip. Timing was of the essence. Let's assume that we are in a part of the Pacific where, at a certain time of year, the wind blows from the east 70% of the time. For the other 30% it is variable between northerly, westerly and southerly. This is where local knowledge comes into play. Your *waka* is loaded up, your crew is fit and ready to go. One morning at first light you stand on the beach and look out over the reef. You have no weatherfax, you have no shipping forecast; indeed, you have no radio. But the stormy season is just about over. The moon has been growing bigger by the day and that will help you see the horizon and the pattern of the swells by night. Now the wind has turned in your favour; how long will it stay that way?

You go and seek out Old Matagi, the navigator who taught you almost everything. He scratches his grey hair, squints at the sky and nods: 'Five days,' he says, 'maybe six.' Enough you think, and run back to the beach. Even allowing for the westward current pushing you back 15 to 20nm each day, this wind will take you 500 miles to the east, perhaps 700 if the wind stays strong. Then, after searching an area across the original course and when the wind has reversed, it will be favourable for a swift and safe run back to your home island.

If, on the other hand, the journey has been travelled before, there may be a map. Old Matagi will draw it on the sand for you to memorise. He will use shells to represent the islands, use sticks of wood to represent the swell and the likely direction of the wind at that time of year. It is thought unlikely that such flimsy devices were taken on board boats, but they were certainly used for educational purposes.

Captain James Cook and Sir Joseph Banks were impressed enough with the capabilities of Tupaia that they recruited him to the crew of the *Endeavour*. Five years later, in 1774, a Spaniard called Andia de Valera also spent some time on Tahiti. Amazed by the way in which the Polynesians readily undertook the often-lengthy voyages between their islands, he came to this conclusion:

> When the night is a clear one, they steer by the stars… not only do they note by them the bearings on which the several islands with which they are in touch lie, but also the harbours in them, so that they make for the entrance… and they hit it off with as much precision as the most expert navigator of civilized nations could achieve it.[21]

Señor de Valera may be over-egging the pudding here. On a number of occasions Tupaia told Captain Cook that he was going to take him to a particular island, and he did. But sometimes it took a little longer or a little further than he had predicted, so it seems likely – if not fortunate – that he was using a different navigation technique to get them through the reef! Once the island had been found, and that meant you had to be able to *see* it, he would use pilotage methods, basically using his local knowledge and eyeballing the way in.

However, that is not the issue. We know that Tupia had a 'chart' of Polynesia in his head, but he also knew what Banks called the 'bearing' for each of his 70-plus islands. Tupaia, though, didn't have a magnetic compass; so how was that bearing expressed? And remember that he didn't just know the bearings from Tahiti, but most from each island to the other islands. In other words, if you stand on any one of the 70 islands (let's call it), there are 69 'bearings' to the other islands. That makes a grand total of up to 4,830 bearings if you include the reciprocals!

Tupia and his fellow-navigators had remembered more than the 'passage-planning chart' of Polynesia. They had also memorised the layout of the stars in the night sky – and the way in which the sky related to the chart. I hope you are mightily impressed!

# The Vikings

## THE NORSE SAGAS AS CRUISING GUIDES

*My mother told me men*
*Must and would buy me a good*
*Fast ship and finest oars*
*To fight with Viking men;*
*To stand tall in the prow,*
*To steer the vessel well,*
*To hold for harbour and*
*Hack down man after man.*[22]

Egil Skalla-Grimsson, *Egil's Saga*

THE VIKINGS were really a kind and gentle society of farmers, maligned and misunderstood by history – or so my Scandinavian friends tell me, contradicting their own sagas. Their main claim to fame is that Leif Eriksson discovered North America centuries before Christopher Columbus fetched up in the sunny climes of the Bahamas – or so my Bahamian friends tell me. The truth is that there is no archaeological evidence that the Norsemen wore cattle horns sticking out from their helmets and they didn't make their ocean voyages on rafts; not even the late Thor Heyerdahl made that proposition. The Vikings travelled in fine longships which, although sturdy, had very low freeboards and were notoriously wet. The not very funny joke at the time was that you needed a man bailing for each man rowing.

Longships were square-rigged when the wind was favourable and rowed when it wasn't; which is much like many sailors today – sails up when off the wind, engine on to windward. The Norse boats were steered with a 'steering oar' or 'steering board' fitted to the right quarter of the vessel, thus giving rise to the term 'starboard' for the right side of any boat. The rowing configuration combined with a keel-less hull made it possible to beach the longships or to probe a long way up rivers, and they put this to good use. They could even drop the mast and drag the boats overland, if need be.

The Norwegians claim that the Swedes drive their Volvos down the middle of the road in order to avoid the wild flowers at each side. This is clearly libellous, but it is certainly the case that the Vikings from what is now the Swedish part of

Scandinavia considered rivers adventurous enough and headed east across the Baltic Sea to establish trade routes south down the great Russian rivers of the Volga and the Dnepr. The cities of Kiev (in the Ukraine) and Novgorod stand where the Vikings first camped. It is said that they eventually reached as far south as Constantinople. What they had to trade was valuable iron ore, a mineral later to have great significance in ocean navigation.

The Danish branch of the Viking family were early visitors to British shores but, clearly deciding that the climate was little better than that at home, headed further south around France and Spain before entering the Straits of Gibraltar and 'gunk-holing' their way around the north-west coast of the Mediterranean as far as Italy. They still do this today, travelling a few weeks each summer by Boeing or Airbus and staying in the best resorts. These Danes were, by all accounts, coast-huggers and rarely ventured much beyond sight of land – except to invade England. The first well-recorded assault on the British Isles was against a monastery on the island of Lindisfarne off England's north-east coast. This was not an attempt to open up trading relations, but a deadly marauding raid aimed at thieving any riches accumulated by the monks. It took place in 793 CE and was certainly not the first incursion. This kind of thing was the dark side of Viking expansion and probably misrepresents the genuine intentions of the majority of the community in its need to settle new land and trade whatever goods they had to offer.

Norway's Vikings can lay claim to being the best seafarers. They headed west and, apart from southerly excursions to explore Ireland (founding the capital city of Dublin) and the west coast of Britain, managed to settle Iceland and Greenland – but failed to make any long-term impression on what was to become Canada and the United States. With some justification, they called the Atlantic Ocean 'the Norwegian Sea' (see top of Fig 1.1).

It is believed that the Norwegians discovered Iceland in 860 CE; 90 years later, some 10,000 Norse people had settled there. Given the size of the longships, that represents a considerable number of voyages across a somewhat hostile ocean. It has to be said here, though, that some would accuse them of being fair-weather sailors who only set sail in the summer. Others, me included, would suggest that they were just being sensible. One of these settlers was Erik the Red, who was so-called because of the colour of his hair rather than the colour of his hands. It could have gone either way because Erik was what the FBI would call a 'fugitive from justice', being on the run after killing someone in a fight back in Norway. In 982 CE, while in Iceland, Erik killed again, suggesting that the 'Red' part of his name might also refer to his fiery temper. Unable to head back to Norway, he set off towards the west and discovered a huge, desolate and mountainous landmass. He probably thought that such an achievement would get him off the murder charge and, after three years, went back to tell the folks in Iceland all about it. Erik called the place Greenland, and with this bit of marketing 'spin' ('green' is not the first word that comes to mind when you think of Greenland) he encouraged a new wave of Norse migration.

Erik had a son called Leif Eriksson who obviously didn't want to be known as 'Erik the Red Jr', but did want to be known as a navigator. Leif had heard about another Viking who had been blown off-course while sailing from Iceland to Greenland. In about 992, Biarni Heriolfsson fetched up at a likely-looking land-mass but, finding it seriously short of Norwegians, concluded he was in the wrong place. Instead of staying on and usurping Christopher Columbus as the historic-ally recognised European discoverer of North America, he shrugged his shoulders and waved the crew and passengers back into the boat. Hearing this tale, Leif Eriksson decided he would upstage his dad and Biarni and discover America prop-erly. He set off in 1002 CE and probably landed on what is now Newfoundland. The story goes that Leif called it 'Vinland' because a German crew member wan-dered off one day and returned drunk, a condition he put down to eating the wild grapes; if we are to believe this, the fruit must have been fermenting on the vine.

Most of this transatlantic exploration happened between 800 and 1100 CE – a much shorter period than that of Polynesian expansion, but mightily impressive none the less. The tales related above are mostly from the Norse Sagas. These were written hundreds of years after the events they described and it can be assumed that they included a considerable amount of colour and spin. However, their descriptions of Vinland's geography are correct and the essential veracity is under-scored by modern-day archaeology, which has identified Viking settlements as far south as New York. The only remaining mystery is why the Vikings decided to leave – did the Native Americans take a dislike to these unwanted guests? What the whole era proved was that these early Norwegians had mastered the funda-mental rule of navigation for ocean explorers: can you find your way back again?

## THE POLAR STICK

Polaris clearly played a starring role in Viking navigation. Weather permitting, the Pole Star was clearly visible well above the horizon along their favourite latitudes; starting at Sogne Fjord, 62°N was an invisible Route 66 passing north of the Shetland Islands, south of the Faeroes and leading west all the way to the south-ern cape of Greenland. Such latitude sailing was critical to the extent that if you were heading for Iceland it would be preferable to start further north on the Norwegian coast, maybe from Trondheims Fjord at 64°N. It's important to note of course that Erik the Red didn't think of this passage as '62 north' or whatever; he was no better at spherical geometry than the Polynesians. But he did need a reference point to know he was on track and that job fell to the Pole Star.

It seems unlikely that the Norsemen made much use of the fist of Kaho's apprentice (see pages 51–3). That technique worked for the Micronesians and Polynesians because, when they could see it at all, Polaris was low on the horizon. For the Vikings, it was relatively high, far too high to be stacking one hand over the other to achieve a guesstimate of 62°. It does seem probable, therefore, that they devised one of the earliest mechanical navigation aids: the polar stick. Such a thing would be about as simple as it can get; hold a stick of wood vertically so that the top touches the Pole Star. If the horizon bisects a notch lower down on the stick, then you are at 62°N, more or less. The stick could be calibrated with a number of notches – not marked 62°, 64°, of course, but marked for the sea route followed on that latitude. And it needn't be a stick – notches cut on the mast would do the job almost as well (and you'd be less likely to lose it).

There has been some speculation that the Vikings also used a knotted string to do this job. Tying the knots with any degree of accuracy would seem to be something of a challenge but, when weighted at the end, the string should hang reasonably perpendicular to the horizon. You can also hang it conveniently from your belt, wear it around your neck or tucked away in your pocket, should you have one.

## SOL-SKUGGJÁFJØL: THE SUN-SHADOW BOARD

Today's celestial navigators use a sextant to measure the altitude of the sun, moon, a star or a planet, and from that – with the use of a lot of tables and some calculation – can estimate the position of a boat at sea. The easiest of all these is the 'noon sun shot', which is exactly what it says, a sextant shot of the sun at midday. On long voyages this is often the *only* sights taken by the navigator. Each day, at noon, he will get a position from the sun; but obviously, the closer he gets to land, the less lazy he can afford to be. The method is called 'sun-run-sun': run for 24 hours, take a sun shot, run for another 24 hours. It seems that the Vikings used a similar method, although without any means of accurately measuring the time, it gave them a latitude but no longitude.

The Sol-Skuggjáfjøl or 'sun-shadow board' makes use of the fact that the sun provides an indication of its altitude whenever it casts a shadow (see Fig 1.4). The designers of sun dials made use of this fact as a means of telling the time. The Vikings applied it differently; for a given time of the year, the shadow could be used to estimate the latitude of the boat. Now keep in mind that the Vikings had not acquired the concept of 'latitude' in the sense that they understood 'number of degrees above the Equator'. What they *did* understand was that 'if you leave Trondheims Fjord heading due west and do not drift too far north or south, you will reach Iceland'. This they could check by reference to the North Star using a polar-stick or a knotted string. But could the sun be used to re-check latitude in the middle of each day?

The life of the Vikings was very much dominated by the behaviour of the sun. They knew that, each winter, the sun would do little more than scud along the horizon in its daily passage from dawn to dusk. This meant gloomy days and long, dark nights. As spring led to summer, the sun would rise much higher in the sky;

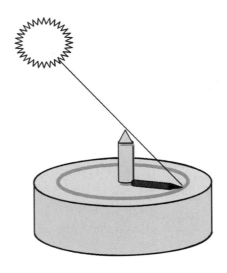

**Fig 1.4** The Viking sun-shadow board.

but never exactly overhead that far north. Clearly, then, the time of year would be a factor in using the sun's shadow to get a latitude. This was dealt with in the design of the 'instrument' they used: the sun-shadow board. The shadow was made by a wooden peg in the middle of a board: a 'gnomon'. The gnomon was adjustable according to the time of year. In the summer, the peg was set high. In the winter, it was set low. That makes sense, doesn't it? If the sun is low, the shadow from the point of a high-set gnomon would go right off the board.

Obviously, the Vikings didn't get involved in a lot of trigonometry when making a sun-shadow board. So, from a practical point of view, how did they go about it? This is my speculation. First of all, you need to be in the right place, specifically the departure point to follow a latitude to, say, Iceland. A Viking navigator has a basic sun-shadow board and late one morning he sits in a sunny spot overlooking Trondheims Fjord. He needs to know when the sun has reached its highest point – noon. He pushes a stick into the ground and, using a plumb-line, checks that it is dead vertical.

Now he sits back and can relax for a while because he has brought his apprentice navigator with him. Every few minutes, the young cadet places a small stone at the end of the shadow made by the stick. A length of twine with a few knots in it helps him to determine when the shadow is at its shortest point. As soon as the shadow is the same length on two measures, he wakes up the navigator and shows him. The older man pats his head encouragingly and picks up the board. Holding the piece of wood as level as possible, perhaps by using the horizon, he adjusts the height of the wooden peg until the shadow reaches halfway across the flat surface of the board. He quickly makes a scratch at the end of the shadow and on the stick (the gnomon) at the point it enters the hole in the centre of the board. The first part of the task is done.

The apprentice watches as his mentor loops a length of thread around the peg and, using a sharpened iron nail, scores a circle around the board, the radius of which is exactly the same as the length of the shadow. Then the navigator removes the peg and cuts more notches in it below the point he made when he marked the shadow. It is now spring and, as the longboat progresses towards its destination the peg will have to be pulled out a little every few days to keep it accurate. The youngster will travel with him for the first time and he will teach him that when the shadow is outside the circle the vessel is too far north, and when inside, too far south.

There is a practical issue with the use of this instrument: the need to keep the plane of the board horizontal. It is said that the Faeroe Islanders used such devices until the 19th century and their solution was to float the board in a tub of water. I have my doubts about the effectiveness of this in anything other than a dead calm sea. A more sensible approach would be to suspend a pendulum arrangement from beneath the board and to let it swing. This idea was used a few years ago when a Scandinavian group tested the practicality of the sun-shadow board at sea: the recommended pendulum was a beer bottle – half empty, of course.

Did the Vikings develop more sophisticated versions of the Sol-Skuggjáfjøl (sun-shadow board)? Perhaps by adding additional circles for other useful latitudes? They may have done, but as Version 1.0 seemed a success, there may have been little motivation to make it any fancier. If you want to try, see Part 3 for some ideas on how you can make your own board.

## THE UUNARTOQ COMPASS

Much has been made of a small scrap of wood discovered during an archaeological excavation in southern Greenland during 1948. A Danish researcher was digging in the ruins of a convent near Uunartoq Fjord when he discovered that it had been constructed on top of another building. He continued excavating in what proved to be a site dating to 1000 CE and unearthed a number of wooden artefacts.

One of these appeared to be a fragment of round disc-shaped object with notches along its edge (see Fig 1.5). By chance or design, the notches correspond to the points of the compass from just west of north to just east of south. There are also a few faint scratches on the face.

It was not long before there was speculation that the discovery was a 'Viking sun compass'. Not all academics fell in line with this conclusion, pointing out that farmers used a variety of improvised sun dials to indicate the passage of the seasons. What you see in Fig 1.5 is a modern 'spin' on the artefact; it is the original piece of wood embedded in a modern compass rose. The notches could match the points of the compass by chance – it might just be an ornament of some kind.

'Dances with Elks' and my other Norwegian friends will forgive me if I declare my lack of conviction. Maybe I will reconsider if more complete examples are found.

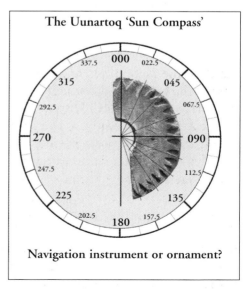

The Uunartoq 'Sun Compass'

Navigation instrument or ornament?

**Fig 1.5** The Uunartoq compass.

# Pharaohs and Phoenicians

*I built you ships, freight ships, arched ships with rigging, plying the Big Green [Sea]. I manned them with archers, captains and innumerable sailors, to bring the goods of the Land of Tyre and the foreign countries at the end of the world to your storage rooms at Thebes the Victorious.*

Ramses III (1197–1166 BCE)

## KING NECHO'S BIG ADVENTURE

UNTIL THE RENAISSANCE, when science began to prevail over super-stition, the eastern Mediterranean wasn't just the centre of the Earth, it was the centre of the Universe. And Ramses' 'foreign countries at the end of the world' were little more than neighbours; it was a much smaller perceived world, but not one without ambition.

As early as 2900 BCE journeys of exploration were made to the Land of Punt (or Pwanit). Punt is somewhere down the Red Sea; sorry to be vague, but some archaeologists believe it to be on the Arabian peninsula (in other words, the north-east coast of the Red Sea), others lean towards it being further south on the Horn of Africa, possibly on the Indian Ocean side. There is also evidence that it could be as far south as Dar-es-Salaam; *pwani* is the Swahili word for 'coast' or 'shore'. If this mysterious land was what we now call Mozambique, it was a long trip, over 4,000nm, but not one that represented much by way of a challenge to navigation. Getting to the Red Sea itself was another story. Wood and other materials had to be transported overland so that boats could be built at Kosseir for the voyage south.

One reason we know so much about the ancient Egyptians is because they recorded their history and culture on the walls of buildings and tombs, thus giving accounts of their civilisation a certain perpetuity to anyone with a pick and shovel. In this way, seafarers would have known about the reefs of the Red Sea and the prevailing weather conditions would influence their strategy for a voyage to the south. From June through September, brisk northerlies would have promised a fast and lively passage south. At this time their boats were not unlike Viking longships: a high prow, flat bottom and a square sail set on a deck-stepped mast. For pilotage and going to windward, these 25m-plus boats could carry 20 or more oarsmen. From January through May, the winds are southerly and slight and this is where the rowers would play their gruelling role in getting the cargo-laden craft back to Egypt. When out of sight of land, the sun and the stars would have helped them hold a course.

It was worth the trouble because the Land of Punt proved to be a source of many valuable and exotic substances such as incense, myrrh, gold, ebony, ivory and different types of wood not available in Egypt. In 1493 BCE, Queen Hatshepsut dispatched five ships with 30 rowers in each on a shopping trip to Punt. Inscriptions on the walls of her temple near Luxor in the Valley of the Kings record that the ships returned 'laden with the costly products of the Land of Punt and with its many valuable woods, with very much sweet-smelling resin and frankincense...'23 If the Egyptians rounded the Horn of Africa, there is no reason to believe they didn't sail further down the coast of East Africa. But did they circumnavigate the whole continent?

For much of this period, the Mediterranean world was dominated by the Greeks and the Phoenicians (from the part of Syria now called Lebanon). The Greek domain stretched through most of Turkey, the Black Sea, the Baltics, mainland Italy, southern France and half of Sicily, while the Phoenicians had most of Cyprus, the coast of North Africa, southern Spain and the other half of Sicily. But where were the Egyptians? Apart from a later excursion overland through the Sinai to Palestine, they were not big on maritime empire-building and the historical consensus seems to be that they had little enthusiasm for sea-faring; much of their boatbuilding and navigation skills they borrowed from other nations. In which case, how did they manage to get out of the Red Sea and head south? Well, it seems they subcontracted the expedition to the Phoenicians.

It is unclear why King Necho II (or Nekhau, who reigned between 609 and 594 BCE) decided that it would be a good idea to sail all the way around Africa – or 'Libya', as it was then known to the Egyptians. It may be that he was trying to capitalise on the success of the trading missions to the Land of Punt. It could be that he saw the Greeks and Phoenicians prosper from their domination of the Mediterranean and thought that such an expedition would lead him to lands that *he* could conquer. The story is told by a Greek writer called Herodotus of Halicarnassus:

> [Africa] is washed on all sides by the sea except where it joins Asia, as was first demonstrated, so far as our knowledge goes, by the Egyptian king Necho, who, after calling off the construction of the canal between the Nile and the Arabian gulf [Red Sea], sent out a fleet manned by a Phoenician crew with orders to sail west about and return to Egypt and the Mediterranean by way of the Straits of Gibraltar.24

If Punt really was as far south as modern-day Dar-es-Salaam, then at least the first leg of the voyage would have been familiar to the expert Phoenician sailors. Herodotus tells us how they made out:

> The Phoenicians sailed from the Arabian Gulf [the Red Sea] into the southern ocean [Indian Ocean], and every autumn put in at some convenient spot on the [African] coast, sowed a patch of ground, and waited for next year's harvest. Then, having got in their grain, they put to sea again, and after two full years rounded the Pillars of Heracles [the Straits of Gibraltar] in the course of the third, and returned to Egypt. These men made a statement which I do not myself believe, though others may, to the effect that as they sailed on a westerly course round the southern end of Libya, they had the sun on their right – to northward of them. This is how Libya was first discovered by sea.[25]

If the sailors really did claim that they had seen the sun on their right hand, then that is convincing evidence on its own that the circumnavigation really took place. Herodotus' reaction in saying that he did not believe that part of the story has to be read in the context of contemporary ignorance about the world being round.

Just as the first leg of the passage down to 'Punt' would have been familiar, the same might be said of the final leg. It's hard to believe that the Phoenicians had seen the Pillars of Heracles without venturing out of the Mediterranean and taking a look up the Iberian Peninsula and down the coast of West Africa. There is even speculation that they reached as far south as the mouth of the River Gambia. At some point heading north they must have had their hearts lifted by the sight of a familiar headland, bay or coastal settlement.

Herodotus was writing some 200 years after this expedition took place and there does not seem to be any archaeological evidence – such as a discarded oar or a broken water vessel – to confirm that it ever actually happened. But who could have imagined that the sun would arc through the sky on their right as they sailed west around the cape unless they were actually well south of the Equator? And the idea that they stopped off every year for some agricultural bunkering has a certain boring practicality to it. I'm prepared to believe it could have happened and, if so, full credit to the Phoenicians for their seamanship and to pharaoh Necho for his sponsorship; it was a feat not repeated until Vasco da Gama sailed the opposite way from Portugal to India 2,000 years later.

## LATEEN RIGS AND WIND COMPASSES

The early square-rigged vessels used by the Vikings, the Phoenicians, the Greeks and the Arabs shared a serious limitation: the direction of the prevailing winds in the region dictated their navigation strategies. The movement of goods and people in the Mediterranean and the Red Sea was seasonal, the direction of movement being determined by the direction of the wind. Fig 1.6 shows a typical wind compass dating from the early Renaissance. Earlier ones have been found carved on the walls of buildings near harbours.

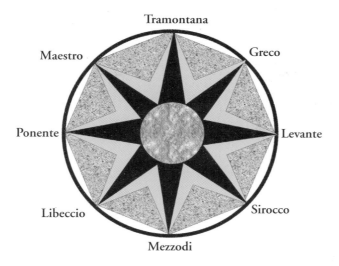

**Fig 1.6** Early renaissance wind compass.

Each point of the compass was covered by a seasonal wind and you would not depart for your destination port unless you were certain you were going to sail with the right wind on your stern or quarter.

The dominance of the winds faded somewhat with the introduction of the fore-and-aft lateen rig. (The word 'Lateen' is a distortion of 'Latin', implying Mediterranean.) This innovation liberated seafarers and made it possible to progress against the wind. The navies of the European empire-builders were relatively slow to adopt the idea. The larger ships of the line still relied heavily on square sails for running downwind, but the addition of fore-and-aft foresails and mizzens improved performance across the wind.

We should note that the wind compass is *not* a navigation instrument, but a way of representing information. It is still used in a refined and compact form on pilot charts to indicate the direction and strength of winds throughout the oceans.

# The Arabs

## SHIPS OF THE DESERT AT SEA

THE REST OF THE ARAB WORLD picked up where the Egyptians and Phoenicians left off. The difficulty of travelling across the terrain made it inevitable that the Arabs would make extensive use of the Red Sea, the Mediterranean, the Persian Gulf and the Arabian Sea for regional trade. Unlike their forebears, they regularly voyaged to India and South East Asia; the only question that is still open is, did they make it around the corner to China before the advent of Islam in the 7th century? The evidence is tenuous and the earliest clue, from a Chinese writer, is dated 671 CE:

> In the beginning of the autumn… I came to the [province] of Guangdong, where I fixed the date of a meeting the owner of a *Po-sse* ship to embark for the south… At last I embarked from the coast at Guangzhou [Canton]… [for Sumatra].26

The case here swings on the belief that '*Po-sse*' is the Chinese transliteration of the word 'Persia'. Whenever they started, the passage to China was a considerable undertaking. A contemporary account of the seamanship of Captain 'Abharah said this about him:

> He was well-versed in the ways of the sea and made the voyage to China seven times. No one had crossed to China before him except as a perilous adventure. No one had ever been heard of who had made the voyage without accident and returned: if anyone made the outward voyage safely, that was a wonder, and a safe return was rare; and I have never heard of any but him who made both the outward and return journey wholly without mishap.27

With a combination of bad weather, difficult seas and hoards of pirates, the voyage probably never got much better.

Were the ships up to it? The archetypal Arab craft was, and still is, the dhow. These sturdy wooden craft vary in length from 15m to 40m and are characterised by the single large fore-and-aft triangular sail that we conventionally call the 'lateen' rig. Earlier boats were known to be square-rigged, rather in the fashion of the Viking longships, and the switch to the lateen configuration would have considerably enhanced their windward capability. That alone would have extended their operating range. It has been pointed out that lateen-rigged boats have difficulty tacking, and larger vessels 'wear round' by turning 360° to windward. This is not possible, however, in restricted waters. I once crewed in a dhow race, and when we needed to go about, a nimble crew member scampered up the mast and pushed the spar vertical so he could kick it around the mast.

Dhows were strong but heavy and slow – 5 knots being considered impressive. I found a recent visit to a small harbour in the Gulf quite sad; the only masts were radio masts and beneath each deck was a very large Perkins diesel, sometimes two of them.

## THE RAHMĀNI AND THE KAMAL

To an extent, you would expect the people of the Middle East to be good navigators. Much of the region is covered by featureless desert that in many respects always reminds me of the sea. Nomadic tribesmen can read a lot into what – to my humble Occidental eyes – seems to be a characterless terrain (as can the Inuit with snow). For example, sand dunes have shapes formed by the wind and that particular shape can tell you from which direction the wind has been blowing – a bit like ocean swell, really, but more slow-moving. Combining this observation with knowledge of the seasonal patterns of prevailing winds can then give you an idea of direction.

But the Arabs' great achievement has been in astronomy. It is still the case that the skies have a breathtaking clarity no longer available in more northern, industrial climes. The sand might lack detail, but the night sky never does. This achievement was driven not just by commercial and survival imperatives to be able to navigate across the desert, but by a religious demand to know the direction of Mecca. There is indeed a reference to astro-navigation in the Koran:

> 'And He it is Who has made the stars for you that you might follow the right way thereby in the darkness of the land and the sea; truly We have made plain the communications for a people who know.'[28]

As the content of the Koran dates from the 7th century CE, this certainly marks the Arabs as early users of the stars for wayfinding. Certainly they were pioneers in the science of astronomy and George Hourani records that observatories were established in cities such as Damascus and Baghdad, and by 830 CE Ali ibn-Isa had written his astronomical treatise.[29] The astrolabe was also invented in this part of the world.

An important innovation was the *rahmāni*, a book that combined sailing directions and astronomical tables. These books contained information about coastlines, reefs and winds as well as a rough guide to trading ports throughout the region. The roses on their charts (introduced before the end of the 10th century) had 32 points to represent 15 stars (rising and setting) in relation to north and south. This might not have taken things as far as the Polynesians' memorised sequences of rising and falling stars, but was much more accessible to the journeyman seafarer by virtue of being written down. In the context of committing crucial information to memory, it is worth noting the use of 'pilot poems', verse used as a means of remembering sailing directions for specific voyages. One of these guides the skipper down the East Coast of Africa.[30]

Hourani's scholarly book is definitive about one technique common to the Arabs, the Vikings and the Polynesians: 'Latitude was determined by the height of the sun or the pole star, which were measured by a primitive finger-system.'[31]

The use of the hand to estimate elevation was somewhat supplanted by a little basic technology. The *kamal* was a rectangle of wood to which was attached a length of string knotted at strategic points. Each knot represented a significant latitude; not necessarily 10, 20 or 30°N, but possibly the latitude for a destination port or a headland where a turn was required. The device was used by gripping

**Fig 1.7** Exploration and trading routes of Arab seafarers.

the relevant knot between the teeth and extending the piece of wood until the string was taut. When the *kamal* fitted exactly between the horizon and the Pole Star, you were on your target latitude! Add a little polish and a word or two from the Koran and you had the perfect seafarer's talisman.

The introduction of the magnetic compass as a navigation aid resulted from Arab trading contact with China. The earliest records of its use date from the late 11th century when it was employed by Arab and Persian trading ships operating between the Middle East, India, Sumatra (Indonesia) and the port of Canton (Guangzhou) in South China (see Fig 1.7). Compasses were not considered particularly reliable and were only used on rare occasions when the night sky was obscured. There is a good case for arguing that the magnetic compass found its way to the Mediterranean and Europe by way of Arab sailors. There is no record of astrolabes being used at sea by Middle Eastern seafarers, but they were certainly used on dry land because *rahmāni* included latitudes for each port that was likely to be visited.

# The Chinese

## SAMPANS AND JUNK HISTORY

I HAVE TO DECLARE a particular interest in Chinese seafaring. I have travelled the country extensively and have stood on the Bund in Shanghai and watched junk-rigged boats and powered barges ply the river. In Hong Kong I have hitched rides on some of the few old cargo 'junks' that still operate in the mouth of the Pearl Delta. The rigs that characterise maritime China have been disparaged in the age of the Bermuda rig. Here, however, is an alternative assessment:

> …a sail plan that uses fully-battened lug-sails on an unstressed rig, sometimes on a partially stressed rig. Of oriental origin, a junk-rigged vessel has certain marked advantages: it is self-tacking (indeed, self-gybing); can be reefed by easing off the halyard; can be un-reefed by hauling on the halyard; can be patched without affecting performance; does not require replacement sails and attracts attention when entering a new anchorage. Probably the best rig for single-handing and has excellent down-wind and cross-wind performance, but is pretty pathetic when beating to windward, rarely managing better than 45°.[32]

That assessment is based on personal experience; I once owned the port half of a 55ft junk-rigged schooner. The sea-going craft are not to be confused with the *sampan*. These are flat-bottomed boats used on the rivers and in the harbours of China and some other countries in the Far East. Sampans are usually rowed or sculled, invariably by a woman as old as Confucius' mother, a cigarette stuck to her lower lip and working a *yuloh*, a sculling oar, over the stern. I have seen the boats fitted with small inboard engines, the transom being too high for an outboard. The name is a distortion of the Chinese *san pan* or 'three planks', which implies that the construction was based on a carvel-built hull of three planks which curve up towards a high bow.

I am describing this special interest in Chinese history and culture in order to stress that I approached Gavin Menzies's book, *1442: The Year China Discovered the World*,[33] with much enthusiasm. For those of you who were at sea when the 544-page book was published in a storm of publicity in 2002, here is the abridged version.

Zheng He (1371–1435 CE) was a favoured eunuch in the Ming dynasty, so favoured that he was made admiral of the fleet. Between 1405 and 1430 CE he commanded seven major voyages. Most historians and archaeologists accept that Chinese merchant mariners sailed throughout the Indian Ocean as far as the east coast of Africa and across South East Asia, perhaps reaching as far as the north-west coast of Australia. But Gavin Menzies, a former Royal Navy submarine commander, wanted to take things much further than that; on the sixth of these voyages, he decided, the Chinese rounded the Cape of Good Hope and headed up the coast of West Africa to the Azores, then across the Atlantic to Venezuela. Here the fleet divided, one-half going north through the Caribbean to Rhode Island before circumnavigating Greenland and returning home via the Barents Sea and the Bering Strait. Meanwhile, the rest of the fleet was heading around Cape Horn and up to California (where they introduced the horse to North America) and west across the Pacific, dropping in at most of the islands of Polynesia along the way. According to Menzies, the world is strewn with artefacts proving that all this really happened.

The fleet was huge – 300 junk-rigged vessels carried some 27,800 people and thousands of horses and other livestock; it must have looked like a scene from the movie *Waterworld*. The ships of the line were over 100m LOA and carried 1,000 crew and passengers. By comparison, Columbus' *Santa Maria* was barely more than 20m in length, and he had an easy job, it seems, because he was navigating from charts incorporating the pioneering discoveries of Zheng He and his admirals. Sadly, my enthusiasm for this remarkable tale was soon dampened; none of the evidence stands up, and that which is presented in the book is distorted to fit the author's unswerving belief that the Chinese discovered the whole world (in less than three years), but didn't bother to settle anywhere and didn't find anywhere interesting enough to justify returning.[34]

However, tucked in the back of *1442* is an appendix entitled 'The Determination of Longitude by the Chinese in the Early Fifteenth Century': that was something I couldn't ignore.

## LONGITUDE CHINESE-STYLE

I have no doubt that Chinese navigators in the 1400s were as competent as those from the European and Arab worlds; the elevation of the Pole Star would provide a latitude, as would being under a zenith star tracking its way across the night sky (see Part 2 below). Familiarity with rising and setting stars would help the helmsman hold a course. Make notes and draw charts if you ever want to go back again. At that time, these were familiar and well-proven methods. Controversially, though, Gavin Menzies asserts that the Chinese were centuries ahead in the determination of longitude; John Harrison's dogged lifelong commitment to the accurate recording of time was all for nought.

This, in simple terms, is the 'Chinese' system as described in *1442*. An observer who knows his exact position notes a star crossing his local meridian (the imaginary line that runs from north to south celestial Poles through his zenith – the point exactly overhead on the celestial sphere). Let's call that star *alpha*. At the same instant, a navigator who seeks to determine his position notes a star crossing his local meridian. This is star *beta*. Now, if your astronomers have accurately charted the constellations, they will be able to tell you the angular distance between the two meridians on which *alpha* and *beta* sit; that angle is the navigator's *longitude*.

So far, so good. But there are a number of practical problems with this method. The most obvious is this: how do the astronomer and the navigator know when they should be looking upwards for their respective transiting stars? Clearly, they both need to receive a signal of some kind, some distinct event simultaneously visible to both of them. An event that could be seen by both parties to this longitude-finding venture is an eclipse. A solar eclipse (where the moon comes between the sun and the Earth) is no good because it's going to be difficult to see the stars. A lunar eclipse (where the Earth passes between sun and moon) will, however, be seen at night from the shadow side of the planet.

Astronomers have identified four key moments in the process of a lunar eclipse, designated U1 to U4. U1 is when the moon first touches the Earth's shadow, U2 when the moon is fully covered by the shadow; U3 is the moment when the moon starts to emerge; and U4 when it is fully out of the shadow. Menzies proposes that the Chinese convention was to use U3; as the first white sliver appears, the observer back in Beijing and the navigator both look up and identify a star (*alpha* and *beta* respectively) crossing their local meridians. The resulting longitude is measured from a reference meridian of zero at Beijing, a predecessor of Greenwich. So, if our intrepid navigator was somewhere on what is now the coast of Somalia, he should get a result of about 075ºW. Well, he would once he got back to China and was able to compare notes with the astronomer in Beijing! If the angular distance between the meridians wasn't known, they would time it using a combination of 13m high gnomons (shadow poles) and water clocks.

That brings us to the problems with this method. It is certainly a system for calculating longitude, but it is not a practical technique for navigation; it is a survey system that might be suitable for making charts. I say 'might' because there are other fundamental issues that need to be addressed:

❦ Lunar eclipses only occur once every six months or so. (There can be as many as four in a year, but some of these will be partial rather than full.) On a voyage of exploration, how do you know you are going to be somewhere interesting when an eclipse occurs? The longitude of the eastern tip of Somalia could prove useful, some point in the middle of the Indian Ocean less so. And if you miss your opportunity, you have to wait another six months for another chance. What happens if the eclipse takes place on a cloudy night? If this was the method used by the Chinese, how were the navigators of the sixth voyage able to accurately chart most of the world in only three years, as Menzies claims? In theory, at least, they could have recorded no more than six longitudes.

✵ The edge of the Earth's shadow is not sharp. Indeed, the whole process of the eclipse is quite slow. According to NASA the lunar eclipse of 27 October 2004 started at 0114 UT (U1) and finished at 0454 UT (U4), a total of 3 hours and 40 minutes.[35] Accuracy anywhere near 1s is going to be more by luck than judgement.

✵ The local meridian which your chosen star is going to cross is an *imaginary* line. Looking at the night sky is not like looking at a star chart on paper or on a computer screen where the meridians have been helpfully added. Nor is there a helpful dot in the sky marked 'zenith'. In other words, the transit is going to be no more than a guess.

I might have been more convinced by all this if Gavin Menzies had included a world map showing convincing lines of latitude and longitude or at least a few numbers. But those charts, it seems, have all been lost; what Columbus and the other European explorers used were copies. That's unfortunate.

After the publication of *1442*, Menzies must have realised the limitations of this approach and turned his attention to other, more frequent events in the night sky – the eclipses that occur when Jupiter plays hide-and-seek with her four biggest satellites. The difficulty here is that, according to conventional (Eurocentric) history of science, the moons of Jupiter were not discovered until January 1610 when Galileo started peering at the sky through his new toy, a telescope. There were over 1,000 eclipses every year. With one eye on the huge awards on offer to anyone able to devise a reliable method of calculating longitude, the other at the end of his telescope, he burned the midnight oil making sketches, performing calculations and making tables. Once finished, Galileo wrote about his work in a letter to King Philip III of Spain whose offer of a life pension to the winner had lain untouched for 20 years. The king's advisers 'rejected [his] idea on the grounds that sailors would be hard-pressed just to see the satellites from their vessels – and certainly couldn't see them often enough or easily enough to rely on them for navigation'.[36] As if in response to the criticism, Galileo turned his attention to the design of a helmet which could be worn by ship-borne navigators. Called the *celatone* and made from brass, this instrument had a telescope mounted over one eye (for sighting the moons) and a clear hole over the other as a means of ensuring that the whole thing was pointing towards Jupiter. It must have looked something like the night-vision goggles worn by the pilots of Apache attack-helicopters. The maestro sent students off in bobbing boats to check it out but they all returned, no doubt seasick, to report that it was a lost cause.

By the end of the 17th century, the acclaimed French-Italian astronomer Giovanni Domenico Cassini had produced much more accurate tables for the eclipses of what were now called the 'Galilean Moons' and established that they could indeed be used to determine longitude. So, in order to claim that this innovation had been pre-empted by the Chinese at least 200 years earlier, Menzies had to dump Galileo and Cassini in the dustbin of history. One might expect him to claim that the Chinese had also invented the telescope long before the Dutch watchmakers who had been taking the credit since 1608 CE. But he doesn't do that; instead, our intrepid submariner claims that the moons of Jupiter are perfectly visible using the naked eye. Through his website he has, of course, managed to find some people who boast they can do just that. However, I suspect that King Philips III's consultants were right, and defy the *average* person to individually identify each of the moons and to see exactly when the transits occur.

The method did become established and James Cook used it as part of his map-making work, but only on the hard and always through a telescope. He continued to use the technique until he found something better… a good replica of John Harrison's E4 chronometer. This discussion of Gavin Menzies's claims has served as an introduction to my later attempt to propose other methods of determining longitude for the barefoot navigator. When it comes down to it, longitude is about time, and time is about longitude.

## THE SOUTH-POINTING NEEDLE

There seems to be, at least, universal agreement that the Chinese were the first to realise the potential of magnetism in direction-finding. The only dispute concerns when this might have happened. I have seen dates between two millennia BCE and 1040 CE cited, but it doesn't really matter; the Chinese were first, the Arabs got the idea from them, and the Arabs took it to Europe. The compass became the most useful, universal tool in the history of navigation. Most boats have one, and even in today's world of electronics it remains the helmsman's quick point of reference for his heading.

The compass is included in this book because it counts as low-technology, something you can make yourself (see Part 3). What happened in 1040 CE, it seems, is that a Chinese alchemist was trying to turn lodestone (iron oxide) into gold when he discovered that it attracted and repelled other metals. More than that, if arranged to swing freely, it would line itself up in a north–south orientation – and that was worth rushing off to tell the Emperor about. The alchemist must have become even more excited when he discovered that the lodestone could transfer its magic to other metal objects – for example, a needle. Initially this would be placed on a slither of wood and floated in a jar.

It seems, however, that the 'compass' didn't set the nautical world on fire from day one. A chapter from a book written in the 12th century provides an account of trading voyages between Canton (Guangzhou) in southern China and Sumatra (part of modern-day Indonesia):

> The ship's pilots are acquainted with the configuration of the coasts; at night they steer by the stars, and in the day-time by the sun. In dark weather they look at the south-pointing needle.
>
> Chu Yü, *Phing-Chou Kho Than* (Phingchow Table-Talk)[37]

So if all else fails, especially the light, get out the 'south-pointing needle' thing.

The Chinese compass was developed into various fancy configurations; fish, frogs and turtles seemed most popular, but it still floated. The ones that dangled from a line were little better and it was another 400 years before the navigators of China saw a much improved version where the needle balanced on a vertical brass pivot. As with much technology, it improved with travel and the Europeans had refined the compass into a mechanical form that hasn't changed much since the late 16th century.

Probably even more effort was put into resolving the problems of variation and deviation. Those topics are too big to deal with here, so I will refer the reader to Alan Gurney's wonderful book *Compass*, a source that is both informative and entertaining.[38]

## TIMELINE OF NAVIGATION AND EXPLORATION

| | |
|---|---|
| c 2900 BCE | Egyptians make first documented long-distance voyage (down the Red Sea to the 'Land of Punt'). |
| c 2500 BCE | At about this time, the Polynesians begin their migration out of SE Asia towards the east. |
| c 2500 BCE | Early experiments in China for finding direction with magnetism. |
| c 2000 BCE | The mathematics of the Babylonians enables them to predict the motions of the sun, moon, planets and stars. |
| c 1600 BCE | The eastward migration of the Polynesians across the Pacific Ocean becomes more adventurous with much longer voyages being undertaken. |
| c 950 BCE | Phoenician seafarers (from an area now in present-day Lebanon) embark on a trading expedition through the Red Sea. They are believed to have reached as far as the SW coast of India and Sri Lanka. |
| 800–700 BCE | Polynesian explorers reach the Hawaiian Islands. |
| 700–600 BCE | Phoenician merchant seamen explore the Mediterranean Sea and Atlantic coastline south around North Africa and up the coast of Spain. |
| 610–590 BCE | Egyptian King Necho II commissions Phoenician sailors to circumnavigate Africa from the Red Sea, around the Cape of Good Hope and back through the Mediterranean. |
| c 600 BCE | His canal between the River Nile and the Red Sea in disrepair, Pharaoh Necho sends a Phoenician ship to circumnavigate Africa, thinking it will only take a few weeks and will be quicker than fixing the canal. The trip takes three years. |
| 500 BCE | Himilco travels via the coasts of Spain and France to Cornwall in SE England where he establishes the trade in tin. Meanwhile, Hanno settles much of West Africa (as far south as Sierra Leone). |
| 400–300 BCE | Britain and India appear on Greek maps. |
| 275 BCE | The canal linking the River Nile and the Red Sea is reopened. |
| c 160 BCE | Early astrolabe claimed to have been developed and/or used by Greek astronomer Hipparchus in Alexandria. (See also 1050 CE.) |
| | |
| 1 CE | The Polynesians have reached as far east as Fiji by this date. |
| 1–100 | Earliest date for the Chinese invention of the magnetic compass. Some historians insist that the marine compass did not come into play until the 8th century and the 12th century as far as the Europeans and Arabs were concerned. |
| 120 | The mathematician and astronomer Ptolemy (Claudius Ptolemaeus, 90–168 CE) publishes his 'world atlas'. Ptolemy proposed that all other celestial |

| | |
|---|---|
| | objects circled the Earth. His maps included lines of latitude and longitude and involved a number of different projections which enabled the curved surface of the Earth to be represented on a flat surface. |
| 500 | Pacific migration has now reached as far east as the Marquesas and Society Islands. |
| 600 | Pacific migration extended as far north as Hawaii. |
| 700 | The Polynesians are thought to have reached Rapanui (Easter Island) by this date. Unless some of them later made it to Peru, this is the easternmost extent of their remarkable migration. (I have found one source that puts this event as early as 300 CE.) |
| 793 | Vikings raid Lindisfarne off the north-east coast of England. |
| 860 | Norwegian Vikings discover Iceland. |
| 982 | Greenland is discovered by Erik the Red. |
| 992 | Likely date for Biarni Heriolfsson's accidental discovery of North America (Vinland). |
| c 1000 | Around the time of the first millennium an exploration party of Polynesians from Tahiti headed south-west and reached Aotearoa, the 'Land of the Long White Cloud', for the first time. This was the name bestowed by one of the group, Kupe, on the islands we now call New Zealand. In so doing, the Polynesians had completed the population of every inhabitable island in some 30 million square kilometres of the Pacific. As an incontrovertible mark of their seafaring skills, Kupe and his companions were to repeat the trip on a number of occasions. Europe was still in the Dark Ages. |
| 1002 | Leif Eriksson, son of Erik the Red, rediscovers North America. |
| 1050 | Astrolabes first arrive in Europe from the East, probably from Persia (Iran). |
| 1066 | The Norman conquest of England begins. These Normans (Norse Men) are believed to be Vikings who had settled in Northern France. |
| 1100–1200 | The introduction of ship's magnetic compasses in China and Europe. |
| 1271–92 | Marco Polo's epic overland journey to China establishes an essential trade route. |
| c 1275 | Approximate date of the earliest known sea chart, the *Carte Pisane*. |
| 1292 | Marco Polo leaves China by sea and three years later arrives home in Venice. |
| 1328 | The invention of the sawmill encourages shipbuilding. |
| 1372 | Ma He born into a Muslim family in Yunnan, China. He later became Admiral Zheng He. |
| 1405 | Admiral Zheng He (Cheng Ho, c 1371–1435) begins first voyage for Ming Emperor Zhu Di. The 'Treasure Fleet of the Dragon Throne' comprised 62 vessels and reached SE Asia, Indonesia (Java and Sumatra) as well as Sri Lanka. |

| | |
|---|---|
| 1406 | Ptolemy's concept of the Solar System is introduced to Europe. |
| 1409–21 | Zheng He undertakes five further voyages, this time reaching as far as India, the Arabian Gulf, Egypt and East Africa. |
| 1421–3 | Sixth voyage of Zheng He. British historian Gavin Menzies claims to have located wrecks of Admiral Zheng's fleet in the Caribbean after it passed the Cape of Good Hope. However, Zheng is believed to have returned home early from this voyage. |
| 1431–4 | Seventh and last voyage of Zheng He. Some 300 ships and 27,500 men returned to SE Asia and the Indian Ocean. |
| 1432 | Portuguese navigators discover the Azores. |
| 1441 | Portuguese navigators sail around West Africa, reaching the River Gambia by 1446. |
| c 1450 | Prince Henry the Navigator establishes an observatory at Sagres (near Cape St Vincent, Portugal) for the teaching of astronomy, cartography and navigation. |
| c 1450 | Invention of the mechanical printing press enables wide distribution of navigation tables. |
| 1459 | Supposed date of a Chinese chart marking the location of Cape of Good Hope, with detailed notes recording that a Chinese fleet sailed around the Cape (from the Indian Ocean) to reach the Cape Verde Islands. Did a Chinese fleet reach the Caribbean this same year? |
| 1470–84 | The Portuguese explore West Africa's Gold Coast and the Congo. |
| 1488 | Portuguese navigator Bartolomeu Dias rounds the Cape of Good Hope at the southern tip of Africa to enter the Indian Ocean. |
| 1492 | Columbus sails west in a failed attempt to reach the East Indies. But was he armed with Chinese charts showing the American continents? |
| 1494 | The Treaty of Tordesillas divides the non-Catholic world between Spain and Portugal. It is signed by King John II for Portugal and Ferdinand of Aragon and Isabella of Castile for Spain. |
| 1497 | John Cabot rediscovers 'new found land' while searching for the Northwest Passage. He is only 495 years after Leif Eriksson. |
| 1498 | Vasco da Gama reaches the Malabar Coast of India after rounding the Cape of Good Hope. |
| 1500 | Portuguese navigator Bartolomeu Dias dies in a storm off the Cape of Good Hope. |
| 1504 | The City of Venice floats the idea of digging a 'Suez Canal' to link the Mediterranean with the Red Sea and Indian Ocean, thus avoiding the Cape of Good Hope. |
| 1506 | Christopher Columbus dies. |

| | |
|---|---|
| 1511 | Portugal defeats Arab fleet in a major naval battle in the Sunda Strait, taking control of the Spice Islands as the centre of Far East trade. (The Straits lie between Java and Borneo.) |
| 1512 | England starts to build double-decked men o' war. |
| 1519 | Portuguese-born sailor Ferdinand Magellan leaves Spain to circumnavigate the world with 5 ships and 270 men. They winter in San Julián Bay, Argentina. |
| 1520 | On 28 November Magellan's diminished fleet sails into the Pacific to begin the first European crossing of the ocean. |
| 1521 | On 27 April, Magellan is killed by natives in the Philippines. |
| 1522 | On 6 September, one ship and 18 of Magellan's troublesome crew finally return to Spain. Captained by Juan Sebastián del Cano, they were the first Europeans to circumnavigate the world. |
| 1534 | Jacques Cartier enters the St Lawrence River and claims a lot of real estate for France. |
| 1570 | Sir Francis Drake's first Caribbean trading expedition. |
| 1571 | Sir Francis Drake's second Caribbean trading expedition. |
| 1572 | Sir Francis Drake leads expedition against Spanish ports in the Caribbean; destroys town of Portobello and captures Nombre de Díos on Isthmus of Panama. |
| 1577 | Sir Francis Drake sets sail from England to attack Spanish colonies on the west coast of the Americas. He always makes a point of helping himself to superior Spanish charts on any ships he captures. Drake takes the long way home. |
| 1580 | September: Drake arrives back in England, the first English seafarer to circumnavigate the globe. |
| 1585 | Drake heads for the West Indies again and makes more trouble for the Spanish colonies. In 1586 he razes St Augustine in North Florida. |
| 1590 | John Davis invents the 'backstaff' (the 'Davis Octant') and spares the eyesight of thousands of navigators. |
| 1594 | Gerard Mercator dies four months before the publication of his remarkable 102-map atlas of the world. Mercator conceived the map projection that navigators still rely on today. |
| 1596 | Sir Francis Drake dies of dysentery and is buried at sea off the Caribbean coast of Panama. |
| 1609 | Henry Hudson explores a river on the east coast of North America and claims Manhattan Island for the Dutch. He calls it the 'Hudson River'. |
| 1714 | The Longitude Act is passed by the British Parliament. |

| | |
|---|---|
| 1730 | The sextant is invented simultaneously by the American Thomas Godfrey and the British mathematician John Hadley. |
| 1759 | John Harrison completes H4, the first reliable marine chronometer. |
| 1768–71 | Captain James Cook's first Pacific expedition. |
| 1769 | During a visit to Tahiti, James Cook meets a navigator called Tupaia (or Tupia). Amazingly, Tupaia had a detailed chart of Polynesia in his head – an area as big as the continental United States. Not one to miss an obvious opportunity, Cook 'debriefed' him and drew a sketch map. |
| 1770 | Cook charts the eastern coast of Australia. |
| 1772–5 | James Cook's second Pacific expedition. He takes with him a copy of H4. Designated K1 it had been made by London clockmaker Larcum Kendall in 1769. It was to prove remarkably reliable. |
| 1776 | James Cook departs on his third and final Pacific expedition. |
| 1778 | Cook fails to locate Northwest Passage from Alaskan side. |
| 1779 | Cook killed in Sandwich Islands (Hawaii). |
| 1820s | British mathematician Charles Babbage invents the Difference Engine, a form of mechanical computer to be used for the calculation of logarithm tables. The machine was never completed. |
| 1830s | Babbage starts again with the Analytical Engine, a far more advanced, programmable device for the calculation of navigation and mathematics tables. |
| 1884 | The International Meridian Conference agrees on Greenwich as the official 0° longitude. |
| 1973 | The US Department of Defense commissions the satellite-based Navstar Global Positioning System. Does the Death of Navigation start here? |
| 1976 | The replica Polynesian sea-going canoe *Hokule'a* makes the 2,400-mile journey from Hawaii to Tahiti using only traditional navigation techniques. The navigator was Mau Piailug from the Caroline Islands and the expedition was organised by the Polynesian Voyaging Society. |
| 1991 | Working from Babbage's original drawing, a team of British scientists and engineers complete the Difference Engine. It works perfectly, giving accuracy to 31 digits. |
| 2006 | In January, the first Galileo satellite is successfully launched. Galileo is a European venture to establish a civilian global positioning system which is accurate to one metre. <br><br> A Chinese academic announces the discovery of a 15th century map of the entire planet. I remain sceptical. |

# PART TWO

# Practical No-tech Navigation

BAREFOOT NAVIGATION in its purest form is a collection of technology-free techniques based upon observation of the natural world. Environmental factors determine that certain techniques can only be used at specific times of the day. For example, it will be difficult at night to see the shape and movement of the ocean swell unless there are fluorescent plankton in the water or the moon is reasonably full and there are no clouds. Similarly, the stars will be of little use during daylight.

So it becomes clear that, during the main four phases of the day, a specific set of techniques will be employed. It will also be necessary in each of these phases to take some actions that will make navigation in the next phase more effective. At sunrise, for example, a good indication of east can be used to determine the direction of swell and, from that, the angle the boat needs to maintain to the swell in order to achieve the desired course. Table 2.1 shows the relationship between the techniques and the time of day for which they are appropriate.

The letters in the right-hand column are pointers to the relevant subsection in the following part of the text.

*Nothing at this stage demands the use of any form of technology – even something you might have improvised yourself. It is about what you can see and what is in your head.*

### DAWN

| | | |
|---|---|---|
| The Sun | Determine EAST from Sunrise | A |
| The Wind | Check DIRECTION using Sun | B |
| | Check for possible LANDFALL | H |
| The Swell | Check DIRECTION using Sun | C |
| | Check for possible LANDFALL | G |
| The Birds | Check for possible LANDFALL | F |

### DAY

| | | |
|---|---|---|
| The Sun | Backtrack for EAST until altitude reaches 30° | A |
| | Predict WEST once altitude goes below 30° | A |
| The Wind | Use to maintain HEADING | B |
| | Check for possible LANDFALL | H |
| The Swell | Use to maintain HEADING | C |
| | Check for possible LANDFALL | G |
| The Birds | Check for possible LANDFALL | F |
| The Clouds | Check for possible LANDFALL | E |
| The Water | Check for possible LANDFALL | I |

### DUSK

| | | |
|---|---|---|
| The Sun | Determine WEST from Sunset | A |
| The Wind | Check DIRECTION using Sun | B |
| The Swell | Check DIRECTION using Sun | C |
| The Birds | Check for possible LANDFALL | F |

### DARK

| | | |
|---|---|---|
| The Stars | Use Stars to determine COURSE | D |
| The Wind | Use to maintain HEADING | B |
| The Swell | Use to maintain HEADING | C |

Table 2.1

# Which Heading?

## A: THE SUN

### *Rising*

THE SUN is a reasonably precise indicator of direction for up to two hours after sunrise and for less than two hours before sunset. Between those two periods the sun is too far away from the horizon to be able to make accurate projections back to where it touched the horizon or forward to where it will sink below the horizon when it sets. Consequently, sunrise and sunset are busy times for the barefoot navigator.

The most obvious use of the sun is in determining the heading of the boat. Just squinting at the sun as it comes up above the horizon tells us the direction of east. (More or less. It's not quite as simple as that, but we'll deal with the variation later.) Once we have east, how does that help us if we want to sail south-east (135º), for example? Well, if we are presently heading into the sun, we need to turn to the right, to starboard by 45°. But how are we going to measure 45° without some kind of instrument?

One crude but simple way of doing this is to use the fact that the width of your clenched fist at the end of an extended arm is approximately 10°. Two fists held together to the right of the sun will, of course, give us 20°. If you then move your left hand over your right and right hand under your left, you will have 40 degrees. Now just imagine an extra half-fist and you have 45°. You also have a feeling that you are going to look pretty stupid standing there in the bow with your arms held out in front of you. With nothing in the distance at 45° that can act as a steering mark, this is not a practical solution. (But for more on measuring angles using your hands, see below.)

The Polynesians had a much more clever answer: they would use the hull of the boat as their navigation 'instrument'. Marks would be carved into the wood that, when in line with the sun, would tell the helmsman that he was steering the desired course. In the case of south-east (135° in modern terms), the appropriate mark would be somewhere on the port side between the bow and the beam. Hawaiian boats were marked up for 16 compass points, each of which could be used in a reciprocal manner giving a total of 32. Even with the best hand on the helm, any more than that would be unreasonably optimistic. On most sailing boats the helm has a whole clutter of standing rigging that she will use instinctively to maintain a course. Once she has established that the sun needs to be bisected by the port shroud, she will use that to keep the boat on the desired course. Even in vessels with compasses, an external fixed point of reference may be preferred, especially when approaching a busy landfall where it is always better to be looking out of the boat than looking down at the compass and other instruments.

Anyway, that's the basic principle of using the sun to determine a heading. There is, however, a complication caused by the fact that the Earth is tilted over by 23.5°. As the Earth orbits around the sun, sometimes the North Pole leans towards it, sometimes away. This causes the sun to appear to rise in a slightly different place each day (between 066.5° and 113.5°) according to the time of year. Twice each year the sun pops up exactly on the Equator at 090°T (degrees true): 21 March and 23 September. After 21 March it crosses the sky at increasingly high latitudes (giving us summer – it can't all be bad news). One month later, on 21 April, the sun is rising 12° further north and, on 21 May, 20° north of 090°, but it is slowing down. Come 21 June it is rising at 23.5° north of true east and that's as far as it gets and starts to reverse. (Note that 23.5° is the same as the Earth's angle of tilt.) By 23 September, the sun is rising due east again and heading south. On 22 December the sun has reached 23.5° south and is ready to head north once more.

The implication of all this, when you are using sunrise to work out where east might be, is that you have to make a slight adjustment for the time of year. For example, if you have just set sail on 15 April, the sun will be rising about 10° north of east. So, as you look at the sun rising, 'true' east is 10° off to the right.

Fig 2.1 shows a schematic designed to make the job of finding east as simple as possible. A similar schematic, Fig 2.2, does the same job for finding west at sunset.

Here is a further thought that you need to bear in mind. The path that the sun follows as it travels across the celestial sphere is called the 'ecliptic'. The ecliptic does not go straight up from the Equator, it heads off at an angle of *up to* 23.5° – does that number sound familiar? This is why you can only use the sun to steer by for less than two hours after sunrise and two hours before sunset, maybe less. Your steering mark is not the sun, but the point where the sun just rose. The further the sun gets above the horizon, the harder it is to project the ecliptic back to the horizon with any degree of accuracy. Once that happens, you have to rely on something else to keep your desired heading; see the later sections on using the wind and the swell.

## *Setting*

The setting of the sun provides navigators with an opportunity to check their course and to re-calibrate the direction of wind and swell.

The sun only sets precisely due west on one day each year; the rest of the year the setting point is somewhere between 156.5° and 203.5°. (It's that infernal 23.5°

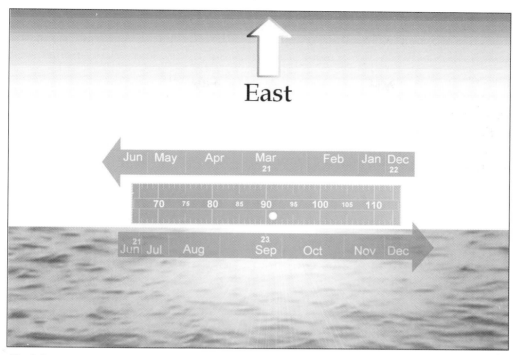

**Fig 2.1** Annual variation of sunrise.

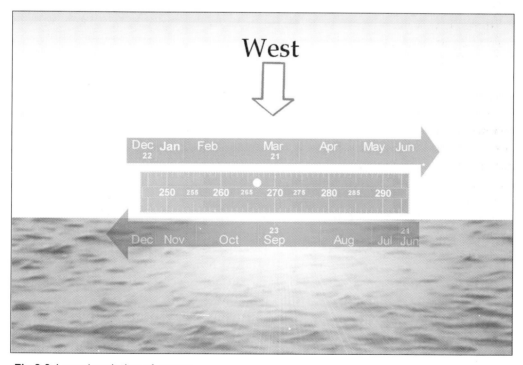

**Fig 2.2** Annual variation of sunset.

precession again. See Fig 2.2.) Exactly how Polynesian and Viking navigators dealt with this remains unclear but, over the centuries, they must have figured out the relationship between the seasons and the sun's rising- and setting-points well enough to be able to make a reasonably accurate adjustment to their headings.

Once the sun dips below the horizon, however, it becomes possible to see some of the stars previously obscured by its considerable daytime brightness. The stars have been there all along; you just couldn't see them while the sun was up. It is the right time of day for our ancient wayfarers (and modern barefoot navigators) to deploy another of their considerable skills – astro-navigation.

## B: THE TRADE WINDS

According to Bob Dylan, 'You don't need a weatherman, To know which way the wind blows', but it might be useful to know *why* it blows and to what extent it can be predictable. Our ancient navigator, now in the bow of his boat, has used the sun to decide where east or west is and, from that, he is going to determine the direction of the wind, the waves and the swell. There might not be a swell, but if there is, he will consider himself lucky; a good swell might give his helmsman a much more reliable reference for the boat's heading. How does the texture of the sea relate to the wind and weather? Well, this is all joined up; the sun causes the wind and the wind causes waves. Strong winds (gales, storms even) cause swell.

It might be a central part of your strategy to sail with or across the wind for a period of time. Rarely is it any sensible person's strategy to sail *against* the wind unless they are racing, or trying to get clear of a lee shore. The wind is the sailing boat's motive power but it also influences, directly and indirectly, the seafarer's navigation decisions. 'Directly' because you might opt for a broad reach for speed and comfort on a long leg; 'indirectly' because what the wind has been doing will have influenced what the sea is doing.

No experienced sailor expects a local wind to be so consistent in its direction that it can be used as a means of maintaining a heading for more than a few hours. At some point it will start to back or veer as the prevailing weather system passes through. The exceptions to this are the Trade Winds; the word 'trade' in this case deriving from the Latin *trado* meaning 'in a predictable or constant direction' and carrying only a fortuitous connotation with merchant shipping in the days of sail. An original barefoot navigator would not have known about the way in which the global climate produces trade winds (and surface currents), but his old mentor would have taught him about the direction and consistency of the winds in their part of the ocean during spring, summer, fall and winter. But even the trades are never consistent all day and every day, so our navigator will use his determination of east as a means of cross-checking that the wind is blowing in the direction it's supposed to be. If it is being contrary, he may have to review his strategy.

Wind is caused by the need for air to move from one place to another, specifically from a place of high pressure to one of low pressure. The tropical zone (between latitudes 23.5º N and 23.5º S) is the part of the Earth most square-on to the sun, so it tends to be hotter than anywhere else. As the hot air expands it rises, causing colder air from the north and south to rush in and fill the gap. The so-called 'sub-tropical high pressure system' results in north-easterly Trade Winds in the northern hemisphere and south-easterly Trades in the southern hemisphere.[39] Where they meet is called the 'Inter-Tropical Convergence Zone' (ITCZ). The influence of the ITCZ actually extends beyond the Tropics of Cancer and Capricorn to as far as 30°N and 30°S. Sandwiched between these is an area known as the 'Doldrums' where the winds are light, variable or non-existent and punctuated by fierce squalls (see Fig 2.3). This is not a place where anyone in a small boat would want to be, but the bands of high cumulonimbus clouds in the distance will give him fair warning that he is getting too close. These clouds are caused by the convection of massive amounts of hot, moist air, but our ancient navigator probably didn't know that.

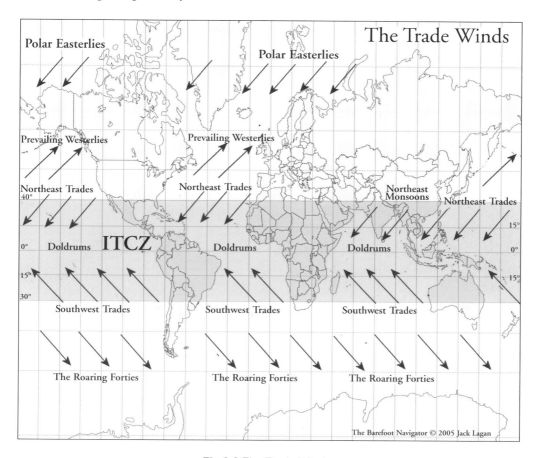

**Fig 2.3** The Trade Winds.

Trade Winds are a percentage game. You can enjoy a 70–80% expectation that they will blow in a certain direction in a certain part of the world at a certain time of year. See, for example, the more detailed charts of Global Wind Patterns for January–February (Fig 2.4 ) and July–August (Fig 2.5). Careful inspection of these charts shows that Polynesia gets much lighter and more variable winds in January and February than in the summer. Although being able to view the overall pattern like this (especially in a survival situation) is important, local knowledge is invaluable. In a non-survival situation you can, of course, buy the 'local knowledge' by acquiring the American or British Pilot Charts for the region.

However, the seafarer must accept that there will be occasions on which he or she will make a whole passage with the wind going the 'wrong' way. But that shouldn't happen too often. Keep in mind that, according to these charts, all Pacific west–east migration was done *against* the prevailing winds, rather suggesting the idea that it all happened as a result of boats being blown off-course was quite wrong.

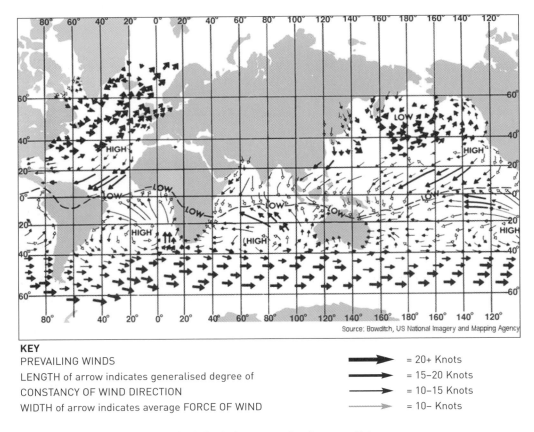

Source: Bowditch, US National Imagery and Mapping Agency

**KEY**

PREVAILING WINDS

LENGTH of arrow indicates generalised degree of

CONSTANCY OF WIND DIRECTION

WIDTH of arrow indicates average FORCE OF WIND

= 20+ Knots

= 15–20 Knots

= 10–15 Knots

= 10– Knots

**Fig 2.4** Global wind patterns for January–February.

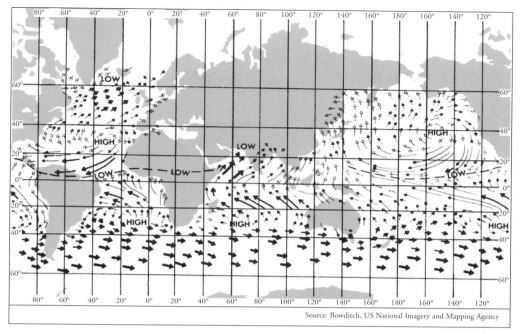

Source: Bowditch, US National Imagery and Mapping Agency

**Fig 2.5** Global wind patterns for July–August.

# C: THE MOVEMENT OF THE SEA

## *The waves*

For dwellers of small islands, the sea is both friend and enemy, a source of sustenance, a source of tragedy. Coping with such a neighbour makes it essential to be able to understand its many moods: the way its surface moves, when that is dangerous, and when it can be exploited.

Waves are the texture of the sea and waves are caused by the movement of air over its surface. It is useful to have a good idea in your head (some might call it a 'conceptual model') of the way in which the sun, the wind and the waves interrelate. The sun heats the Earth's atmosphere. Because the Earth is a sphere, this process is not an even-handed one: in tropical zones, the planet gets full force of the incoming radiation; temperate zones are caught more of a glancing blow and the same amount of heat is spread over a wider area; in the polar regions, the rays of the sun can miss altogether.

The consequences are that some parts of the atmosphere heat up more than others, resulting in a difference in pressure. The nature of physics is that air from the high-pressure areas will try to fill the low-pressure areas in a vain attempt to achieve some kind of equilibrium – a process that gives us wind.

But as the air travels over the surface of the sea it gives us something else: waves. Here's an experiment; the next time you bring your mug of hot coffee up to your lips, blow across the surface and watch the waves. What happens in the environment is merely a difference of scale. In real life, the unhindered wind blowing across the flat surface of the open sea 'picks up' the surface molecules of water, showing as tiny ripples, and the sea begins to get lumpy; if the wind falls, the waves subside again. You never get a helpful Force 5 blowing on your quarter and, *at the same time*, a comfortable ride from a mill-pond surface.

The wind blowing over the surface of the sea is called a 'disturbing force'. Other types of wave have different 'disturbing forces': sub-sea volcanic eruptions and earthquakes are the cause of tsunamis. (*Tsunami* is the Japanese word for 'village' and is so-called because they easily destroy your small coastal community.) Waves themselves can be the disturbing force of other types of wave. A 'seiche' wave is the consequence of powerful waves entering an enclosed area, such as a harbour or nearly enclosed bay, and sloshing about once trapped.

Returning to our surface wind, this kind of disturbing force picks up small waves that are known as 'capillary waves'. This process starts at about 2 knots. As the wind quickens, it is able to get a better grip on the rougher surface and turns the small waves into bigger waves (see Fig 2.6).

From the navigator's point of view, the key element in all this is that the motion of the waves is in the same direction as the wind. Keep in mind that it is the *waves* that are doing the travelling, not the water; the motion does the moving. To convince oneself of this, take a length of line and flick it like a whip. Waves will travel along the length of the rope, but at no time will the rope leave your hand. Similarly, a fishing float will rise and fall as a wave passes it. It does not behave as though you had thrown it into a river where you constantly need to retrieve it and cast it in again, further upstream.

Neither you nor our ancient navigator will be able to observe that, below the waves, the water is tumbling in counter-rotating somersaults. This effect (known as 'orbital motion') only lasts for a few metres and, the deeper the water is, the less effect the waves have on the motion of the sea at the bottom. You can work this out; the circular motion of the waves stops at about one-half of the wavelength (see Fig 2.7 for definitions). So if the wavelength on the surface is 5m (16ft), the water will be decreasingly turbulent down to 2.5m (8ft). Divers returning to the surface are often surprised that the wind has freshened since

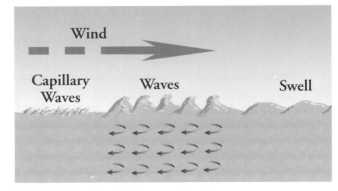

**Fig 2.6** The creation of waves.

they descended and there is a bit of a sea running. Eventually, when the wind speed gets up to 11 knots, it starts to rip the crests apart, causing 'white caps' or 'white horses'. This is the point at which you can determine that you are experiencing Force 4 on the Beaufort Scale. From 17 knots (Force 5) there are even more white caps and spray is being torn off the top of the crests. (See Appendix 9 for the complete Beaufort Scale.)

It is useful to be familiar with the names used for the different parts of a wave and with how a wave is measured. Fig 2.7 shows how the tops of waves are known as the 'crests' and the deepest parts between the crests are known as the 'troughs'.

The 'wavelength' is, as the word suggests, the distance between a crest and the preceding or following crest. The distance between adjacent troughs should, of course, be the same. The talk over a beer in marina bars is usually about wave *height*: 'The crests were ten feet above the main mast!' I can honestly say that I have never heard a yachtsman *under*-estimate the size of a wave, and I include myself in that. (The highest waves I've encountered *must* have been over 50 feet – 16 metres – because I *swear* the crests were well above the top of our 45-ft mainmast…) Anyway, the wave height is the vertical distance between the trough and crest of a wave and is determined by the strength of the wind, the duration it has been blowing over clear water, and by the 'fetch' – the distance over which the wind has been blowing. A very approximate indication of maximum wave height in feet is given by dividing the wind speed in miles per hour by two. (Divide by 10 to convert km/hr to a wave height in metres; see box.) According to the equation, my 50ft waves must have been caused by a 100 mph, Force 12 hurricane! Hmm… maybe the waves were only 25ft high…

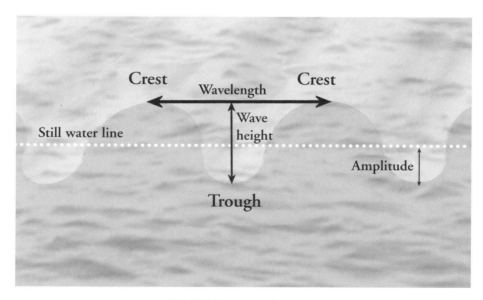

**Fig 2.7** The parts of a wave.

| | WIND | WAVES |
|---|---|---|
| **IMPERIAL** | $\dfrac{\text{Speed in mph}}{2}$ | Max height in feet |
| | 30 mph / 2 = | Less than 15 feet |
| **METRIC** | $\dfrac{\text{Speed in kph}}{10}$ | Max height in metres |
| | 50 kph / 10 = | Less than 5 metres |

'Amplitude' is a technical term that you will only hear oceanographers use; the same applies to the 'still-water line', a notional concept and something that is virtually impossible to estimate in real life. The 'wave period' (not shown in Fig 2.7) is the time in seconds it takes a complete wave (crest-to-crest) to pass a fixed point. As I hope you are never perched on a fixed point, this is not an easy measure to estimate. Related to the wave period is the 'wave frequency', the number of waves that pass a fixed point in, say, 60 seconds. Neither of these values are much use in practical sailing other than to observe that the smaller the period, the higher the frequency, the more uncomfortable will be your ride.

The shape of a wave will give you some clues about its origin. For example, short, choppy seas offshore were probably caused by a recent storm in the area. Longer, steady, waves with a high crest are likely to be much older and may have travelled hundreds of kilometres. Most people will see waves when they finally crash out against a shoreline, maybe even a beach. As the turbulent underside of waves comes into contact with the upward-sloping bottom of the ocean, the front part (or 'face') of the wave is made to slow down. This causes the back part of the wave to catch up and try to climb over the front, increasing the height by as much as 50%. The resulting, *now moving*, build-up of water curls over at the crest and spews plastic ironing boards and young people who talk a strange language onto the beach. This form of wave is called a 'breaker', or 'surf'. When the water from the waves rushes back into the sea, depending on the shape of the shoreline, dangerous 'rip currents' can be formed.

For the navigator, this increased height of a series of waves can be an indication of shallowing and, therefore, the possible proximity of low-lying land and a bar serving drinks. It is also a warning of what to expect when approaching a beach, especially when trying to land in a dinghy. You may be happy with the situation 100m or so offshore, but caution is needed because, in the last 10–20m, the seas will suddenly steepen and try to take control over your planned, orderly, upright landing.

Note that a shallowing bottom can also cause waves to change direction in a process called 'wind refraction'. The line of the waves will turn so that they are more parallel to the shore.

# The swell

We are back on the open sea again and looking at the waves, and thinking: 'If waves are bundled-up energy, what happens to the energy when the strength of the wind decreases?'

Once the wind has dropped or the waves have moved beyond the 'influencing force', the waves are said to 'mature' into a regular pattern known as a 'swell'. In maturing, these waves resolve themselves into groups with similar wavelengths and period (speed). Groups with the same origin and direction are known as 'wave trains'. Unimpeded, waves in the form of 'swell' can travel for many hundreds of miles in the same direction. It is this settled, regular and predictable form of wave that is most useful to the barefoot navigator; its consistency can help him to hold a course. The origin of a swell can be somewhat random: five days ago there was a storm somewhere to the south. But the origin can also be predictable to an extent; the north-east Trade Winds of the North Pacific are known to generate a north–east swell.

(Be alert to a long-standing inconsistency in the way navigators describe the direction of things. Winds are described in terms of the direction from which they originate. This is also true of sea and swell. It is not true of a sea current, which is always described in terms of the direction in which it is moving.)

During daylight and moonlight, the helmsman will be able to angle his bow to the wave train in order to keep a reasonably steady course. Some Polynesian sailors were able to do this 'by feel', an especially useful skill during overcast nights. That is not quite as awe-inspiring as it might at first seem. If your heading is opposite to that in which the swell is travelling, the swell will lift your bow, perch the boat on its crest and then let you down, pushing the stern up as it passes. Then it will do it again. And again. And again. The movement of the boat – and the balancing movement of your body – will fall into a pattern. If the wind shifts and the helmsman turns a little off the swell, the boat will start to roll a little, introducing a corkscrew motion that will be immediately noticeable; you are off-course.

For the man or woman on the helm, two swells are definitely not better than one. Cross-swells caused by conflicting disturbing forces make this form of steering very difficult, as do waves caused by a local surface wind working across the direction of the underlying swell. In such confused seas, and in the absence of any other clues to direction, the helm can do no better than struggle to keep any kind of straight course. (For the good news, see 'Reflected and Refracted Swells' in the section on Landfall.)

Although our Polynesian wayfinders would have been more than happy to find themselves on a friendly 'sea-farers' swell', we can be confident that they would have taken every opportunity to check its direction. If they are far enough north, a quick glance at Polaris will help; if far enough south, a glimpse of the Southern Cross would help to reassure them. Dawn, dusk and a noon sight of the high sun would all serve to provide what the good navigator yearns most: a cross-check on his previous calculations. There is, however, another reason for these frequent verifications. Such is the reliability of swell that a shift in direction can only really mean one thing – the influence of a nearby land mass. We will deal with that phenomenon in the later section on landfall.

## *Currents*

If there is a current in the direction you want to travel, take it. It will give you a free ride at 2 or 3 knots and hundreds of long-distance rowers can't be wrong. In other words, if you have limited motive power, surface ocean currents should play a major part in your navigation strategy. This is especially true if you are in a survival situation.

Any water that is moving – tides or currents – is described in terms of its 'set' and 'drift'. 'Set' is the direction *towards* which it is moving. 'Drift' is its speed. There are two types of ocean current, those driven by the wind and those caused by temperature and salinity differences. The latter are called *thermohaline* and are somewhat analogous to the way air shifts around in the atmosphere. As you would expect, all wind-driven currents are *surface currents*, as are some thermohaline types. However, in the expectation that you are not cruising in a recycled U-boat, we can now forget about this distinction and just concentrate on what is happening where the sun shines.

Here is a simple example of currents providing both a problem and a solution. If you want to sail from Florida to the Bahamas, it is a good idea to start from Cuba. The speed of the Gulf Stream heading north for its Atlantic crossing is usually between 3 and 5 knots. ('Stream', by the way, is another word for 'current'.) Even in a powerful sport-fishing boat this can't be totally ignored, and knowledgeable locals advise against attempting the crossing from northern Florida under sail. The easy solution is to take a leisurely cruise down the Intra-Coastal Waterway to, at least, Lake Worth and then head east from there. But the locals will also tell you about a weaker *inshore current* which has a southerly set. There are more brownie points (but fewer beers) for using this as part of your strategy.

*Periodic currents* are tides – in other words, movements of waters influenced by the moon and the sun. Tidal flows can often be faster than ocean currents. The tidal flow along the south coast of Scotland in the Solway Firth can exceed 4 knots. This is great if you are heading for Ireland but, unless you time your return for the ebb, it is not a good idea to return that way if you are sailing. Fortunately, from this point of view, tides become less and less of a concern the more offshore you are. In some waters they are not really an issue at all; the Mediterranean and Baltic Seas being cases in point. (See Appendix 12 for a chart of world ocean currents.)

Bad weather in the form of long periods of powerful winds can change the set and drift of whatever current you have been sailing on. As you would expect, wind-driven currents will tend to be heading in the same direction as the prevailing wind for the area in which you are sailing. Steady winds away from this direction will change the current. However, such a wind has to blow for a day or more at more than 20 knots for it to make much difference. (Some 3% of the wind-speed is the rule of thumb for the change of drift.)

## D: CATCH A RISING STAR

### *Above the horizon*

Once all sunlight has failed, a Polynesian navigator would need Marama, his Moon God, to illuminate the juxtaposition of sea and sky. A visible horizon is helpful to all navigators because it shows precisely where certain stars are rising and setting and provides the fixed reference point for measuring the altitude of celestial objects such as the Pole Star. The altitude of key guiding stars was the means by which the ancients determined the distance of their boats north or south of their destination islands; the modern barefoot navigator will thinking more in terms of a numerical 'latitude', his or her distance north or south of the Equator.

People in different parts of the world see different parts of the night sky at different times of the year. But the fundamental consideration is the latitude of the observer. Let's start at the 'top' and work down. If you are standing at the North Pole and look above you, you will see Polaris at its *zenith*. (I'll show you later how to locate it exactly.) You are excited because the whole universe seems to be rotating around your head with Polaris as its axis. It is rotating counter-clockwise because, of course, the planet you are standing on is rotating clockwise if you look down. You even forget that you are damned cold.

Now do a Michael Palin and head south – that's any old direction, of course. As you walk away from the North Pole, the stars appear to move differently; now they seem to rise in the east, arc across the sky, and set in the west – just like the sun. The further south you hobble, the more the starry sky follows a huge arc from east to west (see Fig 2.8a). As you travel on to warmer climes, the highest point of this arc moves up and up until, as you cross the Equator, the stars are going right over your head on their nightly journey (Fig 2.8b). But by now Polaris has sunk below the northern horizon. As it did so, Crux has risen above the southern horizon; this is fortunate, because the 'Southern Cross' is going to tell us where south is. (For any navigator, that's as good as knowing the direction of north.) Heading south from the Equator, we have to look over our shoulder to see the stars transcribing lower and lower arcs until, at the South Pole, we look up and see the heavens circling around our head once more.

The way stars (including our sun) appear to move across the sky is fundamental to the job of the barefoot navigator. From the stars we can determine a course to steer; north, south, east and west are relatively easy, other headings are a little more challenging and less universal in application. Stars also help us decide which latitude we are on. Even calculating longitude is not beyond the wit of the average barefoot navigator (well, at least an average barefoot navigator with a quartz wristwatch set to GMT), which is why we will deal with it in Part 3 on Low-Tech Navigation.

All this activity becomes much easier, and much more enjoyable in practice, if the reader takes the trouble to become familiar with the night sky. This can be done by studying one of the many books available on astronomy, and there now seems to be an equivalent number of astronomy programs for personal computers which can be downloaded from the internet. These mostly free programs have the advantage that they can animate the movement of the sky when viewed from any point on the planet. And they can do this in 'fast motion' so you don't have to freeze on deck in less moderate climes. In the tropics, however, I used to lie on deck and watch the magnificent constellation of Orion track across the sky each night from east to west... until I fell asleep, that is. The navigator needs to become familiar with the constellations in order to locate the stars that are going to help him; it is an investment that is worth the effort.

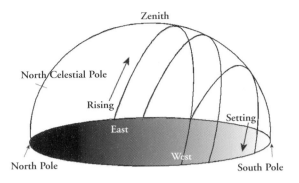

**Fig 2.8a** The path of the stars across the sky from the northern hemisphere.

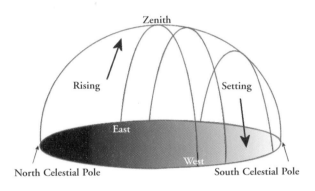

**Fig 2.8b** The path of the stars seen from the Equator.

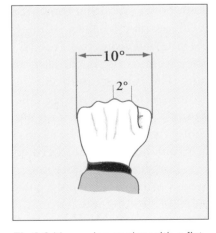

**Fig 2.9** Measuring angles with a fist.

# The hand of Kaho's apprentice: measuring angles

This section of the book concentrates on navigating without technical aids of any kind; but even that style of wayfinding demands the ability to make at least rudimentary measurements of angles. The special knowledge of the ancient navigators was rarely obscure and often very practical. One of the first things that the legendary navigator Kaho would have taught his clever young apprentice was a simple way to measure those angles. Someone once told me this riddle:

> A hand aboard a ship I knew,
> Could measure angles fair and true.
> Without a manufactured aid,
> How were these computations made?

The 'hand' referred to is not a jack-tar but the thing at the end of your arm, and proposes that it can be used as a rough and ready means of measuring bearings and altitudes. I have my reservations about 'fair and true', but this is how it is done.

Stand square-on to where you are looking and extend your arm. The width of your clenched fist gives you an angle of about 10° (see Fig 2.9). Stick your thumb out and you get an extra 5°. This can be used vertically and horizontally of course. An index finger held upright is just over 2° in width; two fingers side by side will give you about 4° of course.

For wider measurements, extend your arm and open your hand wide. The angle between tip of thumb and small finger should be about 15°.

This is all very, er, rule-of-thumb of course, and perhaps we should pause for what my American friends would call a 'reality check'. Trying this on the moving deck of a vessel at sea is at least as difficult as using a sextant. The trick, I have found, is to seize your moment. Your boat rises with the swell – get ready now, keep your eye on the star – then the boat hesitates for an instant before dipping down again. You have no more than a second to make the measurement. As with all these things, practice is the only answer.

As a growing lad, Kaho's apprentice would have soon discovered that the 'instrument' at the end of his arm was less than reliable (and even adults don't always have the same-sized hands). You need to know

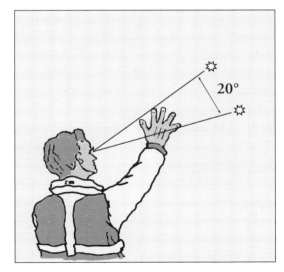

**Fig 2.10** Estimating angles with an open hand.

that, 'my fist is 8°', and 'my extended hand is 15°' or whatever. In order that these odd numbers don't get in the way of the elegant 5, 10 and 15, I always teach crew members to take the measurement in the 'standard' values and then make the adjustment as an afterthought. Like this: 'altitude is two fists, that's 20° (see Fig 2.10). And then: 'But my fist is only 8°, so altitude is 20 minus 2 x 2 equals 16°'. Or, if that arithmetic is a bit challenging, stick with: 'two fists equals 2 x 8 equals 16'. Whatever works for you is fine. (Keep in mind that the ancient seamen, not being into arithmetic yet, would never have refined it beyond 'two fists'.)

Here is a simple way of calibrating your fist using the stars. The angular distance between the second and fourth stars (Mizar and Megrez) in the handle of the Ursa Major (the Great Bear, or the Big Dipper) is, conveniently, 10° (see Fig 2.11). The next time you are in the Doldrums or on the hard, hold up your hand and use that distance to estimate the angle subtended by your fist. Is it ten? Maybe it's eleven? (See below for ways of locating the Ursa Major.)

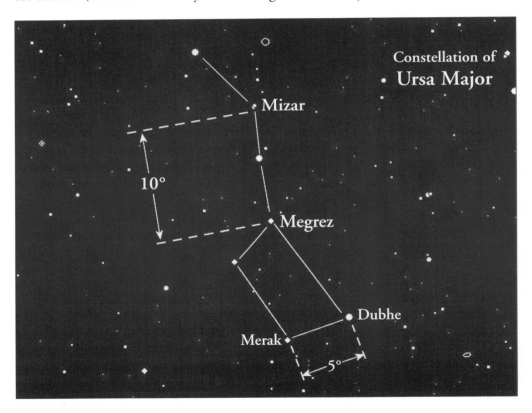

**Fig 2.11** Calibrating your fist using Ursa Major.

In Part 3, I will describe how you can construct a simple 'manufactured aid' from a piece of wood, a length of string and a rusty old bolt.

## *Finding north using Polaris*

Polaris is also called the Pole Star, the North Star and *Hokupa'a* by the Hawaiians. Its use in determining the direction of north was probably the earliest form of hands-on celestial navigation. (It can also be used to find latitude and longitude, but we will deal with these later.) We should note here that when we call Polaris the North or Pole Star, we are giving it a job description. Some 5,000 years ago a star called Thuban (*Alpha Draconis*) held the job of marking the hub of the northern heavens. In 7,500 years time, the task will fall to *Alpha Cephei* in the constellation of Cepheus. For the time being, the barefoot navigator should get to know and love Polaris.

Our first step in finding Polaris is to try and locate the constellation of Ursa Minor, the Little Bear or the Little Dipper. Using some imagination, Ursa Minor looks like a spoon or ladle. Polaris is the last star in the handle. If you are certain you are looking at Ursa Minor, then a vertical line dropped from Polaris to the horizon gives you due north (see Fig 2.12).

If you are not sure you have found the Ursa Minor, then you have a possible double-check if you can see its big brother – or sister – Ursa Major, also known as the Plough or the Great Bear. It is more commonly named the Big Dipper in the USA. I don't really care what you call it; it is far more important to be able to recognise it and to understand how to use it. (The double-checks that follow are also useful when the night sky is partially obscured by cloud. In other words, you might be able to identify Polaris even when the rest of Ursa Minor is obscured.)

The further north you are, the higher is Ursa Major in the sky. Visualising it as the Big Dipper, the handle extends from the left (when it's upright) to the 'bowl' itself. The two stars representing the opposite edge from the handle are called Dubhe and Merak; and they are almost exactly 5° apart, of course! These are 'pointers' because an imaginary line running from them intersects with the Pole Star (see Fig 2.13).

The most important characteristic of Polaris is that it is a fixed star remaining static more-or-less exactly above the North Pole. As the Earth spins, all the northern constellations appear to rotate around Polaris. Even if the Great Bear is standing on its head, it still points to the Pole Star – and that is why identification of this key constellation, regardless of its orientation, is so crucial.

If you can't see Ursa Major, Cassiopeia might be able to help. The constellation of Cassiopeia is roughly opposite the Great Bear on the other side of the Pole Star and at about the same distance. It looks like a big, bright W; if Ursa Major is the right way up (nothing spilling from the dipper), then the W of Cassiopeia will be upside down as you look at it. Start by imagining a line that runs between the end-stars of the W. Then imagine another line running at right angles to that from

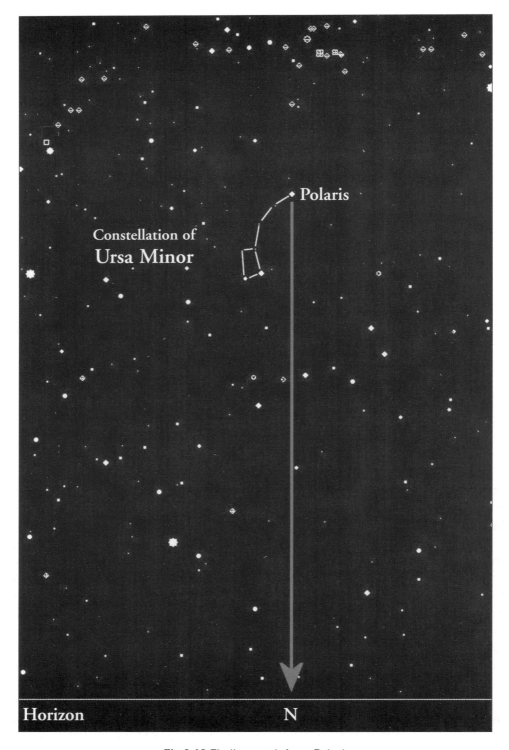

**Fig 2.12** Finding north from Polaris.

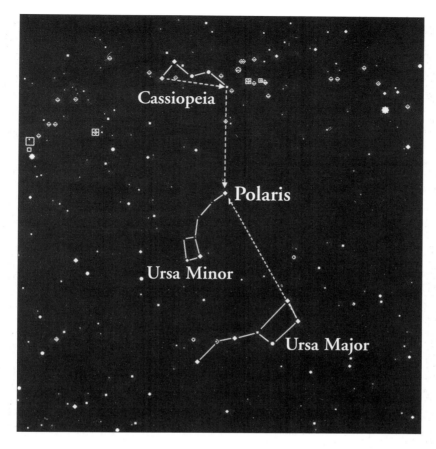

**Fig 2.13** Finding Polaris from Ursa Major and Cassiopeia.

the first star you would touch if you were writing the W; if the W is upside down, it is the one on the right, if it is the right way up, it is the one on the left. That line points to Polaris. It is easier to draw than explain, so see Fig 2.13.

So far, everything seems to be working in our favour; a handy star right over true north and two great big constellations to point at it all night. (There are other pointer stars, but these are the ones that you will use most.) This, then, might be the right time to give you the bad news: Polaris is a second magnitude star (2.1) which means that it is not very bright. It does, however, sit in the middle of the only black patch in that part of the sky. This is the technique: locate Ursa Major or Cassiopeia, follow the pointers until you get to the dark area, and then seek out the Pole Star in the middle of that. A vertical line down to the horizon gives you north. It takes a little practice, but it obviously isn't rocket science.

What can you do if Polaris itself is obscured by cloud? There is a way around this if you can see either of the main pointer constellations. Remember that the angular distance between the pointer stars of Merak and Dubhe is 5°? Well, the distance between Dubhe and Polaris is about five times that – 25°. You should be able to approximate that with your hands to get a rough idea of where the Pole Star is; and if you can guess where Polaris is, you have a rough idea of where north is.

Because Ursa Major rotates around the Pole Star so precisely, it can be used to determine longitude; this is considered in Part 3.

## Finding south using the Southern Cross

In the southern hemisphere, you will be unable to see Polaris. Below the Equator, the Southern Cross is used as a way of finding south. The Cross is located by looking down along the Milky Way until you find a hole. This is known as the Coal Sack. Near the Coal Sack you will find the small but bright constellation of Crux (the Cross, sometimes called the Southern Cross and known as *Hanaiakamalama* by the Hawaiians).

Some care is needed. Ahead of Crux as it crosses the night sky in a *clockwise* sweep is the notorious 'False Cross'. The False Cross is not a constellation, but an unfortunate grouping of stars from the constellations of Carina and Vela. This impersonator is bigger than the original, but to avoid making a mistake you should apply what I can only call a 'cross check'! Following Crux is a pair of very bright stars that point at the Southern Cross; these are called the 'Southern Pointers'. If that does not convince you, look out for a triangle of stars following the Southern Pointers. This is the constellation of Triangulum Australe (the Southern Triangle), more popularly known as 'The Three Patriarchs' (see Fig 2.14). Once you have found Crux and its two fellow-travellers, you should have

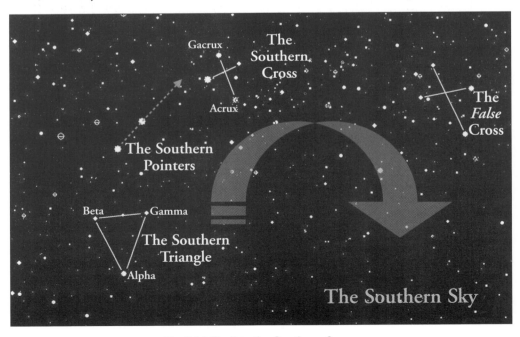

**Fig 2.14** Finding the Southern Cross.

little doubt that you are looking at the correct part of the heavens.

Now another of those reality checks; there is no star in the southern sky that is equivalent to Polaris. You have to visually estimate where the south celestial pole is. You start by mentally drawing a line down the long axis of the Cross from Gacrux (at the top) through Acrux (at the bottom) (see Fig 2.15). This line will lead you to a point above True South, 180°. The point in the Coal Sack that you are looking at is actually the Celestial South Pole. The distance of that from Acrux is five times the distance between Gacrux and Acrux, but the Three Patriarchs (the

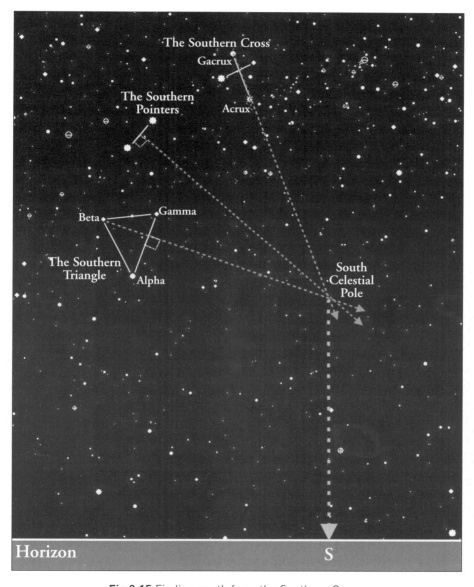

**Fig 2.15** Finding south from the Southern Cross.

Southern Triangle) can make the job a little easier. Astronomers call the three main stars of the triangle Alpha, Beta and Gamma according to their magnitude. If a line between Alpha and Gamma is the base of the triangle, a line from the apex, Beta, which crosses the base at right angles, serves as a second pointer to the South Celestial Pole which is now at the intersection with the line from Crux.

There is a third pointer which, because of its shallower angle, is not quite as satisfactory; but if the Triangle is obscured, you might be forced to use it. The Southern Pointers we used to identify the Southern Cross can also be used to locate the Celestial South Pole. Imagine a line between the two stars and then extend a line at right angles to that. Where it intersects with the line from the Southern Cross is the location of the South Celestial Pole.

True south is vertically down from the South Celestial Pole.

**A final note** As Crux arcs across the sky from east to west, at some point it is vertically oriented. (If you are so far south that you and the penguins can see the full rotation of the southern stars, then there will also be a point when Crux is vertically upside down.) When that happens – and only then – the constellation's pointers are giving you a line right down to the horizon, to due south.

## *Finding east and west using Orion*

Orion ('The Hunter') is a celebrity constellation; it is big, full of bright stars, galaxies and Megallanic clouds (see Fig 2.16). The leading star on its belt, Mintaka, rises almost exactly at 090º and sets almost exactly at 270º. For the purpose of barefoot navigation it is accurate enough to say that the belt of Orion rises due east and sets due west regardless of the latitude of the observer.

If that latitude is 0º – in other words, you are on the Equator – Orion's belt will rise vertically from due east, pass over your head (your zenith) and eventually set due west (see Fig 2.17).

Fig 2.18 also shows Orion rising, but this time from a position 40º south of the Equator. Note that Mintaka, the jewel in Orion's belt, still emerges almost exactly due east but it climbs into the sky at an angle (of 40º to be precise). If we were somewhere in the northern hemisphere, Orion would appear to climb to the right rather than to the left, but the principle is the same of course.

Nearly 12 hours later, Orion will be seen setting in the west (see Fig 2.19). Keep in mind that, the more acute the angle, the more difficult it is to predict the point at which the belt is going to intersect with the horizon. It is generally accepted that the limit is up to two hours of rising and up to two hours before setting. This is true of all situations where you are trying to estimate the point at which a celestial body intersects with the horizon.

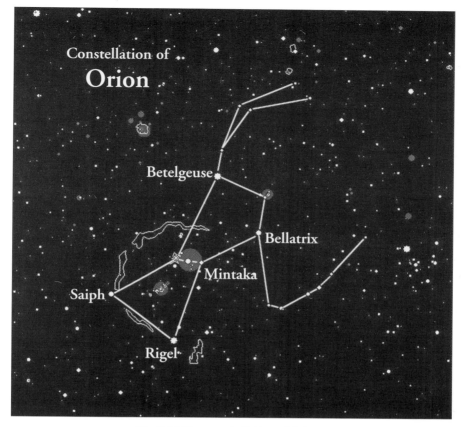

**Fig 2.16** The constellation of Orion.

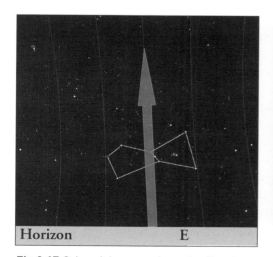

**Fig 2.17** Orion rising seen from the Equator.

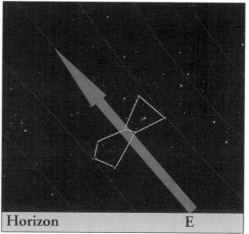

**Fig 2.18** Orion rising seen from a latitude of 40° South.

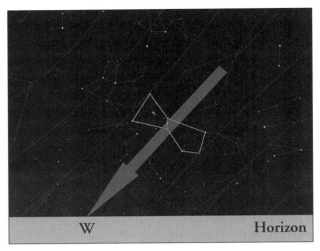

**Fig 2.19** Orion setting as seen from a latitude of 40° South.

## The sidereal compass

If you visit your local chandler and ask for a 'sidereal compass' or a 'star compass', you will get a funny look. A star compass is not something that comes in a nice wooden box and has a needle that points in the direction you need to steer. Nor does it use batteries. For the definitive word on this, we can turn to a real bare-foot navigator, the legendary Nainoa Thompson of the Polynesian Voyaging Society:

> The star compass is the basic mental construct for navigation. We have Hawaiian names for the houses of the stars – the places where they come out of the ocean and go back into the ocean. If you can identify the stars, and if you have mem-orized where they come up and go down, you can find your direction. The star compass is also used to read the flight path of birds and the direction of waves. It does everything. It is a mental construct to help you memorize what you need to know to navigate.[40]

A 'mental construct' is a good way of describing a star compass which, like the wind compass, is a way of representing useful information rather than an instru-ment. Of course, this is a mental construct that you can write down and you are already in a position to make a start. Draw a circle and mark the cardinal points: north, south, east and west. Against north, write 'Polaris' or 'Pole Star'; against south, write 'Southern Cross' and 'Southern Triangle'. Close to east, write 'Orion rises'; near west, write 'Sun and Orion sets'. Now you have a star compass!

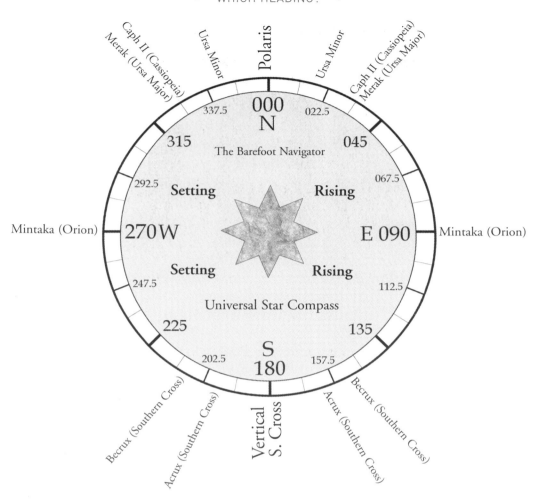

**Fig 2.20** Limited star compass.

Sadly, though, it's not very useful; we could use a good deal more rising and setting stars against the other points of the compass in between those four. Nainoa Thompson says that Pacific navigators remember about 220 stars by name and according to where they rise and set. The star compasses shown on the Polynesian Navigation Society's website[41] are considerably more complicated than a magnetic compass. One major problem is that you don't always get rising/setting stars where you need a compass point. But more can be filled in with what we already know.

Fig 2.20 shows how we can make use of polar stars, at least those which can be seen to rise and fall in temperate latitudes. The star compass you started now looks slightly more useful.

Before we add even more stars we need to consider some practicalities. Here are a few of the problems with star charts:

* They are only useful at night.
* They only work well in the tropics; at higher or lower latitudes, the horizon bearing changes and the angle of ascent narrows (but can still be used for east–west courses).
* They are only useful when you can see the relevant stars.
* Not all the relevant stars rise and set at the same time.
* Many headings will have to be deduced from the available horizon events.
* Away from the Equator, the stars rise and set at an angle that makes it difficult to track backwards or forwards to the horizon.

But it's not all bad news.

Obviously, not all stars rise and set just when we need them, so you have to make best use of whatever the heavens are giving you. If Ursa Minor is not rising and setting (because you are too far north), it provides you with a useful warning; as it swings through about five o'clock you should see Dubhe and Merak (the pointer stars of Ursa Major) begin to appear above the horizon. On the compass I have used Merak because you will be more confident if you see Dubhe first, and then the two of them together. The declination of Merak, its angle above the celestial Equator, is about 56°; so it rises at about 034° on the compass.

After a while, Merak will rise too far to be useful. What are we going to do then? Helpfully, at the opposite corner of the 'dipper' is Megrez, which rises at 033° – close enough. Then, still in Ursa Major, comes Alioth in the handle at 036°. We have just identified what the Polynesians would call a 'star path', and these three would be good for over two hours of steering. All right, they vary by a degree here and there but most helms are happy to work to the nearest 5° (see Fig 2.21).

There is another star path in the north worth mentioning. The lead star of Cassiopeia is called Caph II; it's the one on the right when you look at the W in an upright position. Caph II sets at 329°, but it is soon followed by 27 Cas (the middle star) and 37 Cas (the second left star) which both set at 330°. When the Cassiopeia star path rises again, it gives you a horizon bearing of about 030° (see Fig 2.22).

That, then, is the principle of steering by the stars and the use of the star compass as an *aide memoir*. All we need to do now is fill in some more stars so that we can cover most of the compass points. The Polynesians used about 20 of the brightest stars; Table 2.2 is a checklist of 27. (Horizon bearings are shown to the nearest 1° only.)

Table 2.2 is also useful when looking for zenith stars (see page 67). A generalised sidereal compass based on these stars is shown in Fig 2.23.

Remember that the people of the Pacific had an oral tradition, not a written one like the Egyptians and the Arabs. Nor did they leave much behind that would get an enthusiastic archaeologist excited. I have seen it suggested that the Star

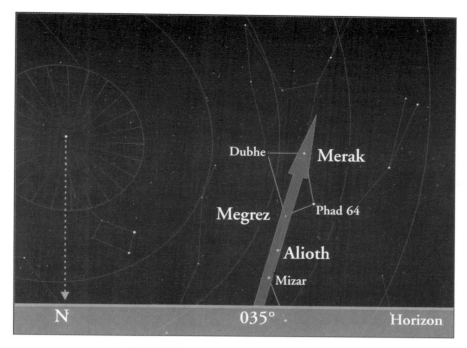

**Fig 2.21** Star path for Ursa Major rising.

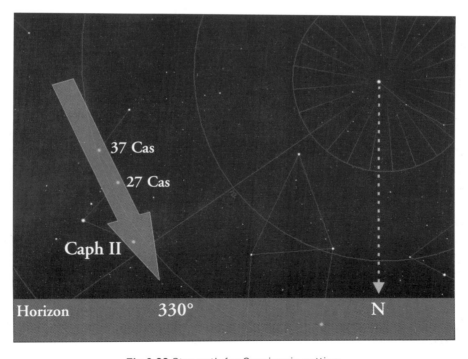

**Fig 2.22** Star path for Cassiopeia setting.

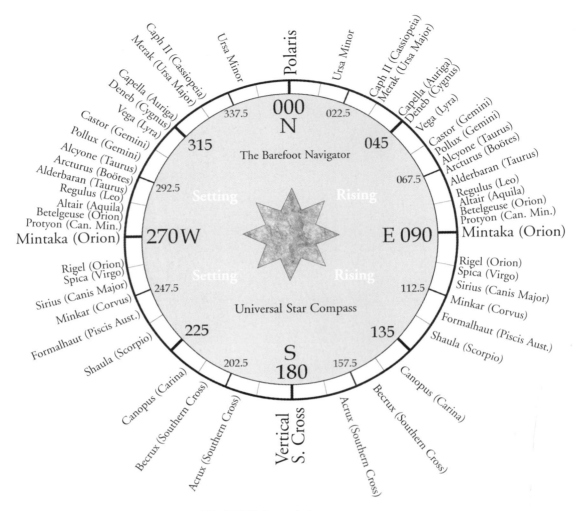

**Fig 2.23** Universal star compass.

Compass is pure speculation. However, I have not seen anyone challenge their charts improvised from slivers of wood and a few shells. Such a thing is a long way from writing of course, but it does suggest an ability to *visualise* what is inside your head. Carving notches on the side of your sea-going canoe would seem to be a reasonable step for Pacific seafarers to have taken. If the helmsman keeps a steeply rising star over a particular notch, he knows he is making the correct heading for that particular leg of his voyage. (Modern-day sailors do this instinctively by lining part of the hull or the standing rigging with a mark.) Transferring those notches to a board makes the navigation system portable between canoes. The possession of such a thing by a navigator would have considerably raised his social standing in an island community. Unlike 'Comfort Zone Navigation', the star compass was for real. We know this because they can still be found in Micronesia, being used as teaching aids for young navigators.

| Constellation | Star | Dec. | Setting | Rising |
|---|---|---|---|---|
| Ursa Minor | Polaris | 90° | 360° | 000° |
| Cassiopeia | Caph II | 59° | 329° | 031° |
| Ursa Major | Merak | 56° | 326° | 034° |
| Auriga | Capella | 46° | 316° | 044° |
| Cygnus | Deneb | 45° | 315° | 045° |
| Lyra | Vega | 39° | 309° | 051° |
| Gemini | Castor | 32° | 302° | 058° |
| Gemini | Pollux | 28° | 298° | 062° |
| Taurus | Alcyone (in the Pleiades) | 24° | 294° | 066° |
| Boötes | Arcturus | 19° | 289° | 071° |
| Taurus | Alderbaran | 16° | 286° | 074° |
| Leo | Regulus | 12° | 282° | 078° |
| Aquila | Altair | 9° | 279° | 081° |
| Orion | Betelgeuse | 7° | 277° | 083° |
| Canis Minor | Procyon | 5° | 275° | 085° |
| Orion | Mintaka | 0° | 270° | 090° |
| Orion | Rigel | -8° | 262° | 098° |
| Virgo | Spica | -11° | 259° | 101° |
| Canis Major | Sirius | -17° | 253° | 107° |
| Corvus | Minkar | -23° | 247° | 113° |
| Piscis Australis | Formalhaut | -29° | 241° | 119° |
| Scorpio | Shaula | -37° | 233° | 127° |
| Carina | Canopus | -53° | 217° | 143° |
| Eridanus | Achernar | -57° | 213° | 147° |
| Southern Cross | Becrux | -60° | 210° | 150° |
| Centaurus | Beta Centauri | -60° | 210° | 150° |
| Southern Cross at 45° | Acrux | -63° | 207° | 153° |
| Southern Cross | Vertical | -90° | 180° | 180° |

Table 2.2

# Where Am I, Roughly?

## LATITUDE: A BELATED DEFINITION

SO FAR I HAVE AVOIDED a formal definition of 'latitude' because the word and the concept are in common use among people likely to be reading this book. However, a more strict understanding will help in understanding some of the barefoot navigation techniques that follow. So, lines of latitude are:

> notional parallel lines of equal angle north and south of the Equator; latitude 0° is the Equator itself, 90°N is the North Pole, 90°S is the South Pole. In modern navigation, latitude is expressed in degrees, minutes and tenths of a minute (not seconds). When combined with a line of longitude, any position on the surface of the earth can be described.[42]

It is clear from this that determining a latitude is halfway towards obtaining a 'fix'. You might ask what good is half a job? Surely that's like the sound of one hand clapping? But a latitude can prove to be very useful when combined with some other piece of navigational information. Some latitudes are inextricably associated with certain locations and we will deal with that idea first.

## ZENITH STARS

In the equatorial region, stars rise in the east and make a beeline overhead for the western horizon. Each one follows its own line of latitude above the surface of the Earth. There are so many stars that there is a good chance that most places of interest to the navigator will have their own 'marker' stars that pass through their zenith each night. Let's take the example of Hawaii. Most of this island chain is between 18° and 23°N. Now it just so happens that the red giant star of Arcturus in the constellation of Boötes tracks across the globe at 19°N and runs directly overhead the island of Hawaii. Therefore, if the navigator is confident that Arcturus is at their zenith, then they can be confident that they are also on latitude 19°N.

The sooner you can make that determination the better, but clearly it is not going to be easy on a boat. I have seen it suggested that a crew member lie on the foredeck with their head against the mainmast looking upwards. (On some boats, of course, there is always a member of the crew in this 'moody place'…) If you are heading east and the vessel is not rolling too much, then watching how the star progresses up the forestay will do the trick. Once it is agreed that you are on the right latitude, the navigator then needs to determine whether the next heading needs to be to the east or to the west. If that is not an obvious decision, then you really are lost.

Fig 2.24 shows the track of some other zenith stars in the East Pacific and the Atlantic. Alderbaran in the constellation of Taurus crosses the surface of the Earth at 16°N, first coming very close to taking you into the port of Curral Velho on the island of Boa Vista in Cape Verde. It then goes on to cross the Atlantic to mark the position of wonderful Guadeloupe in the Caribbean Sea. Further south, Mintaka (in Orion's belt) travels along the Equator, going overhead the mouth of the Amazon before crossing the continent of South America and heading for the Galapagos; here it usefully marks the zenith of Isabela Island. Staying in the Pacific Ocean we can use the star of Rigel (also in Orion) to help us find the Marquesas. Care is needed because Rigel passes overhead tiny Eia, which is actually 70nm north of the main island group.

Let me remind you that the Polynesians were not thinking about the use of zenith stars and latitudes in numerical terms. For them, there was a star called *Hokule'a* (Arcturus) and it was inextricably associated with Hawaii. If your boat was under Hokule'a, then you were on the same latitude as Hawaii and that was it.

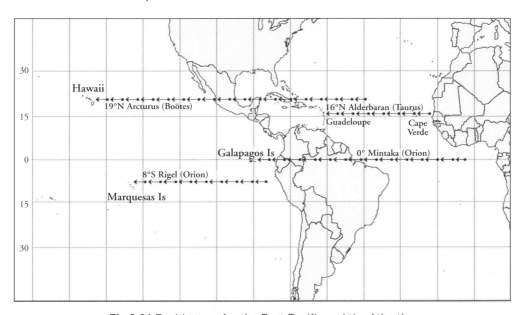

**Fig 2.24** Zenith stars for the East Pacific and the Atlantic.

# USING POLARIS TO ESTIMATE LATITUDE

There are two celestial objects that can be employed to make an estimate of the observer's latitude: the sun and the star Polaris. The Pole Star is by far the easiest option because it commands a fixed position above the North Pole. As the elevation of the sun is constantly changing, a table of its declination for each day of the year is required and this relegates it to Part 3 of the book. (Note that neither work well in equatorial climes and Polaris doesn't work at all in the southern hemisphere because you just can't see it. Seafarers in the tropics, however, have the zenith stars so that might even things out.)

Let's remind ourselves what 'latitude' is. Lines of latitude are a series of notional circles that circumnavigate the Earth and which we use as a guide to navigation. The 'mother of all latitudes' is the Equator which, in relation to the axis of the Earth, represents where a line at right angles to that polar axis touches the surface of the Earth (see Fig 2.25). This – the Equator – is considered to be at 0°. Other lines of latitude are described as being a certain number of degrees to the north or south of the Equator. The 90° lines of latitude north or south have a diameter of zero and are at the North or South Pole.

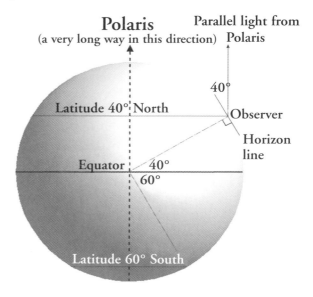

**Fig 2.25** Latitude from Polaris.

So how can Polaris help us to determine our latitude? The first thing we need to consider is that Polaris is a very, very long way from Earth. This has the disadvantage of making it impossible for me to include it on my schematic. The important advantage, however, is that the star is so far away that we can assume that the rays of light radiating from it are actually parallel by the time we get to see them. This means that, wherever we are on Earth, Polaris is always in the same direction – the same direction as the polar axis, if you like. What changes according to our latitude on the planet is the angle of the horizon line where our boat is bobbing about. That is an important consideration; *we* are moving about, not the Pole Star.

In other words, the angle between the plane of the horizon (seeing it as the line where the sea meets the night sky) and Polaris changes according to where the observer is. And that angle is equal to our latitude. Keep in mind that we are dealing with technology-free situations here, so what you are going to get is an *estimate* based on the use of your hands. Much of the history of navigation technology has been about the design and development of devices that will make that measurement more and more accurate. In Part 3 we will look at some devices that you can improvise to do this job but, for the time being, if you can achieve a guess of anywhere near 5° you should be happy.

Crux can just be seen in the south from the lower latitudes of the northern hemisphere, so why not use the celestial South Pole in the same way? As with Polaris, the altitude of the Celestial South Pole above the horizon is the same as the observer's latitude. However, there is no star marking the celestial South Pole for us, so we would be trying to measure the elevation of a black point in the Coal Sack and that can't be good. It can be done, but it is something of a challenge.

From the latitude of Hawaii, the altitude of Acrux is conveniently the same as the distance between Acrux and Gacrux (6°, or three finger-widths). However, from Nuku Hiva, which is 9°S, the altitude is nine times the angle between Acrux and Gacrux – and that's much more difficult to estimate just by squinting at it.

## GIVE ME A LITTLE LATITUDE: A NAVIGATION STRATEGY

'What use is latitude without longitude?' asks the navigator whose pedal extremities are snug inside colourful hi-tech sea boots.

Well, we are not looking for a GPS-type fix. We are looking for something on which we can base a course-planning strategy. Polaris, Crux or one of the zenith stars can be used to give us an approximate latitude. Also, we can point to the very useful fact that latitudes go east in one direction and west in the other; and we know how to find east and west. You might not be precisely aware of where you are on that line of latitude, but you might know where the line will lead you. Let's start with a simple example. You are about to sail home from the out island where you have spent a dutiful few days visiting the in-laws. 'Home' is about five days' sailing to the north-east and you could try it direct, but local old salts have reminded you – as if you needed reminding – that it is very easy to miss. There is no good star on the compass. The low-lying island is not part of a group and has no tall microwave antenna; should you go right past it, trying to find it again could take many days.

So, the strategy passed down through generations is this: 'Go north across the wind for two or three days until you are beneath the path of Rigel in the constellation of Orion. (See Fig 2.26.) Then turn to the east, using the rising and

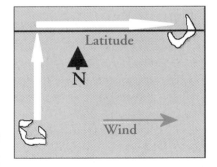

**Fig 2.26** A simple latitude strategy.

setting sun by day and the Southern Cross by night to stay on the path of Rigel. After two days, look for the birds and the clouds to give you landfall.' Doing it this way gives you two easily navigated legs: north, then east. And even if your 'north' is not as good as it ought to be, you are still bound to hit the latitude.

However, without any instruments to measure the altitude of the celestial South Pole and with no means of cross-checking that you are on the line during the main part of the day, there is always a danger that you will drift off-target. The further the destination, the more serious are the effects of being off by a degree or two. So, don't spend two weeks hoping to fetch up at a 200m-diameter atoll using this strategy. The best solution is to island-hop, constructing a voyage from a series of shorter legs, even if it means radically increasing the overall distance travelled. This also has the benefit of enabling you to vary the tactic used for each leg.

In the example shown (Fig 2.27), the distance from Island A to Island B is considered to be too great for a reliable landfall. The indicated route is preferred because it is clearly going to be much easier to make first landfall at Island Group C. After steering due north (with as much westing as you like) to the correct latitude, a turn is made to the left. Overall, a little less time will be spent sailing uncomfortably with

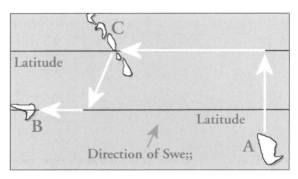

**Fig 2.27** A latitude strategy over multiple legs.

the swell square on the port beam. Once through Island Group C, the new course towards Island B can slightly favour south. This avoids the unappealing situation of being confidently on the right line of latitude, but being uncertain whether to turn west or east. In these circumstances, it could be a long time before the mistake is discovered. It also provides the option of stopping off at one of the islands in Group C if sea conditions look unfavourable for the final leg.

*Avoid making landfall after dark – especially if you are unfamiliar with your destination. Plan the passage to arrive in the morning and, if you are early, heave-to until dawn.*

# Landfall

*Landfall and Departure mark the rhythmical swing of a seaman's
life and of a ship's career. From land to land is the most concise
definition of a ship's earthly fate.*

The Mirror of the Sea by Joseph Conrad, 1903

IT IS A HARD CALL deciding what might be the most exciting part of sailing; is it leaving port for somewhere new, or finally arriving safely and on schedule at that destination? Of course, some seafarers will insist that it is the part of the adventure that comes in between, sailing the ocean out of sight of land.

In the army, old hands advise young platoon commanders never to proclaim that their destination is 'just over the next hill'. The consequences of being wrong are just too demoralising after a long, tiring trek. The same advice applies to navigators, but I have to confess that I can never resist the temptation to declare that 'the twin peaks will appear over the horizon in 15 minutes'.

Landfall is a particularly important aspect of barefoot navigation. The relative inaccuracy of the methods employed has a tendency to make destinations shrink alarmingly. In technical terms, you are dealing with a large 'circle of uncertainty', a circle at the limits of which your target is going to be below the horizon, especially in a small boat. Chance is just as unreliable, so we are going to need all the help we can get and this final section of Part 2 on No-Tech Navigation considers the elements of our marine environment that might point us in the right direction.

## E: THE CLOUDS

Cumulus clouds are formed by columns of warm air rising into cooler air. The sun causes land to heat up more quickly than water and thus starts the process of cloud formation. (It also causes sea breezes, but we will deal with that a little later.)

Such isolated clouds provide us with early pointers to landmasses such as islands; the bigger the cloud, the bigger the landmass. Fig 2.28 shows a rare,[43] perfect example. The cloud is typically cumulus with a flat base and fluffy, rounded white top. It is not moving (take my word for it) and there it is, not showing a shadow on the surface of the sea (which would tell us we had misjudged its distance from the boat. If the direction of the cloud fits with the direction in which we expect the island to be, then change course for it.

**Fig 2.28** Cloud formation over a landmass.

Such marker clouds are not usually so clear-cut and isolated. Expect there to be more cumulus clouds but, in those cases, the marker cloud may be lower in altitude. Sometimes the cumulus is little more than a disturbance in a more complex structure of cumulus and stratus clouds. These might be part of a weather front, but they could be over a much larger landmass, a big island or even a continent that you can't see yet. Have you recently seen other vessels making a course to or from that direction? If you can see a faint blue-green tint to the underside of the cloud, it might be a reflection from a shallow lagoon.

Maybe the birds can help?

## F: THE BIRDS

Before I left the Society Isles I enquired of the inhabitants if there were any islands in a north or NW direction of them, but I did not find that they knew of any. Nor did we meet with any thing to indicate the vicinity of land till we cam [original spelling] to about the latitude of 8° S where we began to see birds, such as the boobies, Tropick and Men of War birds, Tern and some other sorts. [...] [We] saw there many of the above mentioned birds which are seldom known to go very far from land.[44]

*Captain James Cook's Journal*, December 1777

It is interesting how sailors can develop relationships with visiting birds. I remember reading in *The Lonely Sea and the Sky* by Francis Chichester how *Gipsy Moth III* gained an extra passenger during the 1960 Single-Handed Trans-Atlantic Race. Chichester awoke one morning to discover a bedraggled racing pigeon sitting in the rigging. Helping the miserable bird survive became an important factor in sustaining his own morale; the redoubtable skipper had been seasick.[45] The pigeon expired before it was confronted with the challenge of having to explain to a surly immigration officer why it had dared to set claw on American soil without a visa. Chichester went on to win the race in 40 days.

The relevance of this tale lies in the fact that the bird in question was a homing pigeon. It seems as though it had been in one of those international races where the pigeons are driven to France in a special truck and then released to race back to Barnsley or wherever; it must have been blown seriously off-course in a storm. While writing this book I learned two interesting things about these birds. Researchers had discovered that they have magnetic elements of some kind in the area above their beaks. This goes some way towards explaining how they might be able to hold a course. Sadly, though, the discovery contributes nothing towards explaining how they know which course to hold.

The other thing I discovered (2,000 years after Pliny the Elder) was that some seafarers in the northern parts of the Indian Ocean used specially trained homing pigeons as aids to land-finding.[46] The Pacific Tropicbird has similar navigation skills, but it seems a lot of trouble to train these winged wonders for all possible destinations; the idea also implies that you are making routine return voyages to established destinations – trade routes, in other words. You might be 'geographically challenged', but if you have with you a bird that is going to show you the way, then you expect to become lost. It occurs to me though that there might have been something of a support industry for regular maritime traders. I see a pigeon breeder with a cart laden with neat wooden bird cages trundling his way along the dock. Only five groats a bird – a small price to pay for safe landfall. And the product is recyclable – the pigeons that don't make it back, you don't need anyway.

It is in the tradition of Melanesian and Polynesian seafaring that certain birds can provide a reasonably reliable indication of position in relation to land and the direction to steer in order to reach that land. I'm sure, however, that this reference to birds is used everywhere to some degree. It is very much about local knowledge and you don't have to be in the South Pacific for that. For example, tiny Grasholm Island close off the west coast of Wales is home to 30,000 pairs of gannets, probably the biggest colony in the world. These are white birds with dark outer wings and provide great entertainment as they plunge into the sea around the boat. I've seen these handsome birds forage for food some 15 miles offshore and they might go even further. So, any regular sailor or fisherman in the Bristol Channel or the southern Irish Sea will take the presence of gannets as an indicator of the presence of Pembrokeshire almost without thinking about it. (Wales is hilly enough for it to be spotted some distance off, but that's not true in misty conditions; a lack of visibility doesn't seem to put the gannets off though.)

Not all coastlines and island groups have such useful colonies of birds. I once gunk-holed my way around the Bahamas for five months and don't particularly recall seeing a single bird. There must have been some and maybe my powers of observation are waning but, compared with nearby Florida, no measures were necessary to stop birds perching on the crosstrees and using your 42ft pride and joy as a toilet.

The principle of navigation-by-birds is relatively straightforward. Seabirds fly out from their nesting sites in search of food. When they have stuffed enough fish down their gullets, they fly home again. Not all marine birds behave like this; some only nest on land to breed and spend the rest of their time at sea. The albatross is probably the best-known example of this 'pelagic' group and, for navigation purposes, they can be safely ignored.

The birds that do forage from island nest-sites have ranges limited, one assumes, by their power-weight ratio. The benefit of flying further to find more food is cancelled out by the additional energy consumed. But for our purposes, an empirical approach is good enough.

The Pacific is the area in which most research has been done and this substantially confirms my view that local knowledge is essential – to a degree. The best secondary source for bird-range information is David Lewis.[47] He discovered that the consensus of experience throughout the region suggested that relatively few birds provided a reliable indication of the proximity and direction of land.

These are the noddy, the white tern, three variations of booby and the frigate-bird, the street-robber of the seas. We'll look at this group in more detail and see if it is possible to make some generalisations (see the Bird Table).

| THE BIRD TABLE | | |
|---|---|---|
| **BROWN NODDY** | Colour | Dark brown with white head |
| Long wedge-shaped tail. There is also a black noddy, but these feed close inshore from the surface. | Size | Medium |
| | Feeding | Plunge diving on small fish |
| | Range | 20nm |
| **WHITE TERN** | Colour | White all over with black beak |
| Black eye-rings make eyes look larger than they really are. Carries fish sideways in bill. | Size | Small body, long wingspan |
| | Feeding | Dives to surface for small fish |
| | Range | 30nm |
| **BROWN BOOBY** | Colour | Mid-brown, white belly and u/wing |
| Face and bill are yellow in females and light green in males. Feeds singly. | Size | Large (twice size of the white tern) |
| | Feeding | Plunge diving (likes flying fish) |
| | Range | 30nm |

| RED-FOOTED BOOBY | Colour | White with dark trailing wing feathers |
|---|---|---|
| Blue bill and red/brown feet. Young and immature birds have darker, mottled plumage. Feed singly. | Size | Small (about the same as white tern) |
| | Feeding | Plunge dives (stays under a long time) |
| | Range | 50nm |
| MASKED BOOBY | Colour | White with black flight and tail feathers |
| Sometimes called the blue-faced booby. Dives from as high as 30m. | Size | Large (150cm wingspan) |
| | Feeding | Plunge dives for small fish and squid |
| | Range | 50nm |
| FRIGATEBIRD | Colour | Dark, almost black |
| Forked tail and blue/grey hooked bill. Females have white breasts. Scares other birds into dropping their catch. | Size | Very large (230cm wingspan) |
| | Feeding | Scavenge from surface w/out landing |
| | Range | 70+nm |

Lewis learned from indigenous seafarers that the most useful bird of all is the brown noddy. This small, dark-brown bird rarely ventures more than 20nm from land. There is also a black noddy that is no help to you because it fishes from the surface just off the reef and you will have your landfall there. However, the adventurous brown one with the white head and long, wedge-shaped tail flies out from its nesting site in the morning in search of food and heads back to base as the sun dips towards the horizon. While it is at the office, the noddy will circle around at about 10–20m above the surface looking for prey. All these birds make their job easier by seeking out activity by predator fish such as the tuna. These tend to herd shoals of smaller fish to the surface; on seeing this, the noddy will plunge head-first into the water and grab a victim before heading back to the surface.

You will not confuse the noddy with the pretty white tern. This is a much smaller bird that is white overall with a black beak and black rings around its eyes. It has blue feet, but you probably won't be able to see those. The white tern dives too, but only to the surface where it sits ducking under to pick up passing small fry. It will take off again when it realises it is in the wrong place or that it has scared off the cuisine. Crucially, if you see a white tern feeding, you know you are within 30nm of land.

Now for the brown booby – this is not to be confused with the brown noddy or the red-footed booby. The brown booby is a large bird, typically twice as big as the white tern. It is medium-brown with a white belly and white 'arm-pits'. Like the brown noddy, the brown booby plunge-dives beneath the surface. It's not a very sociable bird and is usually seen operating on its own up to 30nm out from its base. (It has been spotted a lot further out, but that's unusual.)

Don't stand with binoculars looking at the undercarriage of passing birds; it's hard to see them on the red-footed booby when it is in flight and, in any case, it is easier to identify from its distinctive white colouring with very dark trailing wing feathers. It's a small bird, about the same size as the white tern, but you won't confuse them when you see them feeding. The red-faced booby dives under the surface and stays under for a remarkably long time as it chases its prey in their own habitat. You may also spot this bird fishing after nightfall. It forages further out than the white tern – up to about 50nm.

The masked booby is sometimes called the blue-faced booby; this is the biggest of the lot with a wingspan of up to 150cm (nearly 5ft). It is white with black flight feathers on the trailing edge of its wings and a narrow, pointed black tail. Juveniles are greyish brown with white patches on their bellies. The masked booby plunge-dives for small fish and squid and often does this from 30m (about 100ft) above the surface. Like the red-faced booby, it forages up to 50nm from land.

The frigatebird is perhaps the easiest to identify. It is a large bird with a black head and black leading-edges to its wings; its tail is split, but not forked. Its behaviour, however, will quickly dispel any doubts about which species you are looking at. The plumage of the frigatebird gets waterlogged, so it cannot land on water. How then does it catch fish? Sometimes it will fly low over the water and scoop dead fish or fragments of fish from the surface without touching down. But mostly it steals fish from other birds. Scientists call this behaviour *kleptoparasitism*.

I have passed many a pleasant hour watching these predators at work. They hover above a flock of feeding birds waiting for one of them to dive. As its target rises from the surface, the frigatebird makes its move. Before the victim gets a chance to swallow its catch, the frigate dives at it aggressively, making it drop the fish in fright. The frigatebird then swoops down to snatch up the fish before it hits the sea again. Frigates often improve their effectiveness by working in pairs; one takes on the job of scaring the fish out of the booby while the other acts as 'catcher'. (Scientists call this *mutualism*.) It doesn't always succeed, of course, but the strategy works often enough for it to provide plenty of entertainment for the passing sailor.

Viewing pleasure is enhanced by understanding that the mutualism extends beyond the birds and shows that frigates do have a positive role to play. Tuna, for example, will chase shoals of prey fish up towards the surface, making them easier to catch. Some will break the surface. Meanwhile, the frigatebirds will be circling overhead, watching all this going on, but unable to take advantage of it. The terns, noddies and boobies will see the frigatebirds circling and fly to the scene and start feeding. Only then will the frigates get their reward. Everyone benefits – except the prey fish, of course. At the end of the working day the frigatebird flies up high to take a look around before heading back to home port. The frigatebird has a range of over 70nm but is most likely to be seen closer in, hovering over a group of conventionally foraging birds – I have even seen them operating in harbours.

What Lewis doesn't mention is the foraging behaviour of birds when pairs are nesting. In these situations one bird has to forage for its mate sitting on the eggs, and it is hard to believe that it will stay out fishing for all daylight hours while its partner goes hungry. Similarly, when the young have hatched, they will be sitting on the nest, squawking, beaks open, demanding to be fed. This suggests that at certain times of the year some seabirds will provide many more indications of direction than otherwise. Clearly, this is a bonus for the barefoot navigator. (However, it may well be that in such situations the foraging range is reduced as a means of limiting the energy expended on flight. It is an interesting balance that the bird has to achieve.)

At the beginning of this section about birds as an aid to navigation, I made the rather obvious point that not all species exist in all locales. As with so much barefoot navigation, local knowledge is a precious asset not usually available to the long-haul voyager. But is it possible to make some generalisations about bird-foraging behaviour that can be used by the navigator – especially in crisis situations? Little has been published about this in the academic press and, by asking questions, I may have planted the idea for a PhD thesis or two. These thoughts are my own, so they come with the usual health warning.

❋ *The smaller the bird, the shorter the foraging range?* This is based on the simplistic notion that lighter birds have less capacity for energy. How big are the batteries in your boat? As big as you can afford, aren't they? But this concept is 'simplistic' because it doesn't take account of the fact that smaller birds consume less energy. Nor does it allow for the frequency of replenishment that might be possible. Further research might prove the generalisation to be correct, but I fret about the *Sterna paradisaea*, the arctic tern. This little bird resembles the white tern, averages 33cm in length, and weighs in at about 300g. Small bird, short foraging range, right? Well, no. The arctic tern, as its name suggests, breeds in colonies in the frozen north during the summer. Then it heads off south to winter in the Antarctic; that's a round trip of over 20,000nm (35,000km) each year. What I need is a smart ornithologist who can convince me that the arctic tern is that exception that proves the rule I'm trying to formulate.

❋ *The more birds feeding at any one time, the closer is land?* From personal (but not very scientific) observation I believe this to be true, especially if the flock you are looking at represents a fair mixture of species. It also makes sense, doesn't it? Birds in mid-ocean are a relatively rare occurrence; most do not venture beyond the continental shelf – in fact, most would not venture beyond the harbour wall if they could get away with it.

❋ *The more frequent the departures from the feeding ground, the more likely it is that the birds are nesting?* The significance of this is that in the breeding season, nesting birds are not likely to venture too far. This could be good news, suggesting that landfall is not too far off.

❋ *Departures in apparently random directions could mean that the birds are looking for other signs of fish – but could also indicate the presence of more than one island?* This sounds potentially confusing if you have to make a decision on course to steer, but that would not be the case if you are expecting to make landfall at a *group* of islands.

Both sea and land birds migrate in fairly predictable patterns; furthermore, *both* seem to migrate in north–south or south–north directions along the coasts of the main continents. More specifically, they seem to migrate over continental shelves, presumably because that's where the best en route feeding grounds are. (Perhaps it is also because, at altitude, they will remain in site of land for most of their journey. This suggests that, in navigation terms, they are 'coast-huggers'. This fact might not provide a precise indication of direction for the barefoot navigator, but it might provide a boost to morale.)

Like all barefoot navigation, the use of seabirds as an indication to the proximity and direction of land is not in any way proposed as a fundamentally accurate technique. In general terms, however, it should be noted that the regular observation of feeding marine birds is good news. The broad reaches of the oceans are not good places for fishing – not enough fish. However, on the continental shelves, the shallower waters, the reefs – that's where fish are found in quantity. And where there are fish, that's where you will see birds trying to catch them. So, this whole bird strategy is only going to be effective reasonably close to land – which is where you want to be.

## *Airplanes*

I know I am going to get some flak from the purists by adding this note, but the word 'Survival' is printed in bold text on my get-out-of-jail-free card. The sighting of an airplane can help give you an indication of position and, near coast and island groups, can assist with landfall in the same way that sea birds and small cumulus clouds do. Just don't tell me that when you are exhausted and low on water you are going to say, 'That plane is not an object of nature – I'm going to ignore it.'

If you see a single-engine, propeller-driven light aircraft flying at about 1,500m (5,000ft) over the Pacific, it is unlikely to be *en route* between Brisbane and Bogotá. More likely, it is island-hopping and, if you have a rough idea where you might be, its course might provide you with some useful confirmation.

Watch the plane carefully. Does it seem to be losing height? Has it lowered its wheels and flaps? Is it turning into the wind? Is it about to disappear below the horizon? Even if it has big floats instead of wheels, there is a good chance that it is arriving at an island you cannot see yet; 'float planes' are known to land in large lagoons. Of course it might be landing on a strip near a mainland coast.

If the plane appears to circle before disappearing below the horizon, that makes sense too. Some small, remote islands are not overburdened with air traffic control facilities, and pilots will fly low over a dirt strip to check that it is clear and to warn any aircraft thinking of taking off that he is about to make an approach. If you see this happen, then you are about to make landfall.

# G: REFLECTED AND REFRACTED SWELLS

If the furrows of the swell you are riding are as straight and even as a ploughed field, enjoy it while you can; it is not going to stay like that. You may get hours, even days, from a really good swell, but eventually it will weaken and get confused. There are a number of reasons for this, some of which can be helpful in detecting the hidden presence of land.

Fig 2.29 shows the prevailing swell on which you are relying for your course becoming confused by another, weaker swell coming from the left. There can be a number of reasons for this. Like the dominating swell, it may have been caused by a distant storm that blew out some days ago; you just happen to be where the resulting swells are intersecting. This information is not much use to you.

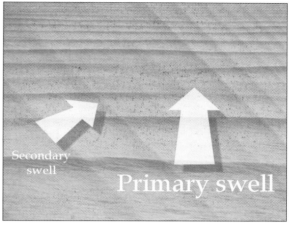

**Fig 2.29** Complex pattern of swells.

What you might actually see coming in from the left, the right, or indeed from straight ahead, is an echo of the swell that you are already sitting on. Like all forms of wave energy swell can bounce off things or be distorted by them in some way. Fig 2.30 shows how a prevailing swell is hitting an island and bouncing back (in a weakened form) in the direction from which it came. For clarity, I have shown the island in the schematic but, if the prevailing swell is strong enough, the reflection will certainly be detectable before you can see the island or headland in real life. Keep in mind, however, that a gently sloping beach is likely to absorb a lot of the energy of the incoming swell and not much will echo back. An island or rounded headland will reflect a swell that is also curved. If your course is taking you some way past the landmass, then the reflected swell will come towards your boat at an angle. This will provide an added clue as to the heading of the island.

As a swell passes along a shoreline at right angles to it, the part of the swell closest to the land will be slowed down and cause the direction of the swell to change and 'wrap around' the back of the obstruction. (You might have seen a line of soldiers trying to turn, line abreast, and keep in a straight line. The soldiers nearest the fulcrum have to mark time while their comrades at the outer end of the 'spoke' have to march faster than usual.) This of course will happen to the swell passing both sides of the island; the two 'refracted' swells will then meet, causing somewhat confused seas.

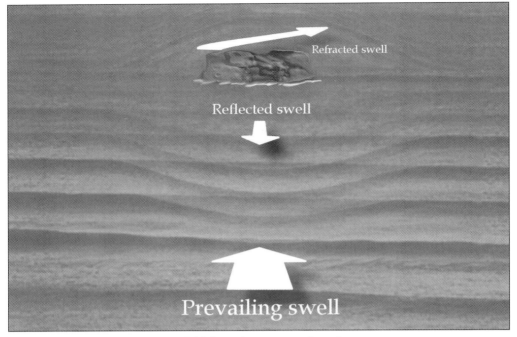

**Fig 2.30** Complex pattern of swells..

A barefoot navigator sailing past this island will get two warnings that it might exist below his horizon. First of all, he will see evidence of a reflected swell. Second, as he passes the island, the secondary coming towards him from off his bow will be replaced by another coming onto his quarter. If this happens, he will begin to worry a little; is he about to miss his destination port? What are the birds doing? Perhaps there is a marker cloud on the horizon?

## H: THE WIND: LAND AND SEA BREEZES

In contrast with the global scale of the Trade Winds, there is a particular type of local wind that is helpful to the navigator expecting to pass close to a landmass or who is hoping to make landfall.

The 'sea breeze' is that cool onshore wind that you might have experienced when standing on a beach or cliff. Like all winds, it is a consequence of the conversion of the sun's energy. As the sun rises into the sky it heats land more quickly  than it heats the sea. This causes heated air to rise and leaves an area of low pressure beneath the rising parcel (see Fig 2.31). The colder air above the surface of the sea moves towards the land in an attempt to 'fill in' the lower pressure. These sea breezes are known to extend anywhere between 3 and 20 miles offshore, depending on the size of the influencing landmass.

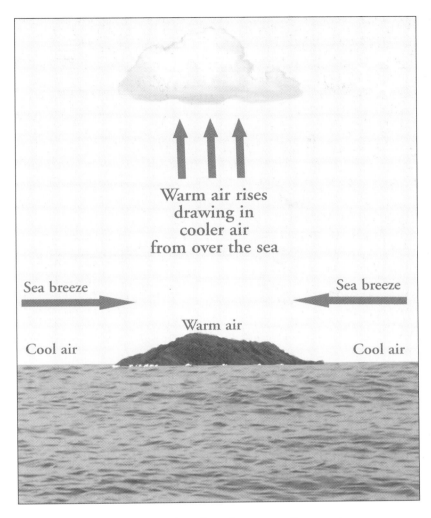

**Fig 2.31** The creation of sea breezes as the sun rises.

How can you determine that you are experiencing a sea breeze rather than just a shift in wind direction? Well, you might be able to see the land – and that is certainly a give-away! Also, if the air that is rising over the land is heavy with moisture, it may well be forming one or more small cumulus clouds, as shown in the schematic. (Of course, you will see the clouds a long time before you see the land beneath them, but you might not be sure that they are marking the presence of an island or coast.)

Another consideration that will confirm you have a sea breeze is the fact that, at night, the breeze reverses direction and becomes a 'land breeze'. As the sun sets, the land cools faster than the sea and the temperature difference reverses. The cooler air over the land then moves offshore to fill the lower pressure area. This causes an offshore wind known as a 'land breeze'.

# I: THE WATER

Perhaps I was being a bit unkind to Kaho, the legendary blind navigator who reputedly could determine the exact location of a boat merely by leaning over the side and touching the water (see Part 1). Maybe he was feeling for weed that had recently blown off a nearby coastline? Unless he tasted the water, then I don't see how he could have been checking the salinity. The other option is the water temperature, in which case he truly did have magical powers to be able to differentiate between the slight rises in temperature caused by the sun warming the shallower water close to land. Maybe he could detect warming caused by volcanic activity on the seabed. (There is another option. In the Irish Sea it might be possible to determine proximity to the coast of Cumbria by determining the level of radioactivity in the water. But that doesn't sound very barefoot to me!)

The colour of the water (unavailable to Kaho, of course) depends on a number of factors. If the sun is low, it will tend to cause reflections off the surface. If it is high in the sky, it will illuminate the bottom of the sea and what is down there will tend to influence the colour. Is it sand, coral, rock, weed? And how deep is it? Mathew Wilson's *Bahamas Cruising Guide* [48] is a superb publication that contains all the usual stuff on passage planning and the whereabouts of the best marinas, bars and restaurants – but it is particularly good on pilotage. This guide has a two-page spread of colour photographs illustrating all the different bottom conditions you are likely to encounter in this part of the world. This is an excellent second-best to local knowledge and I can personally vouch for its usefulness. The Bahamas is very short of aids to navigation; whenever the government gets around to replacing them, they are blasted away by the next hurricane. (I once met an American in a marina bar on Great Harbour Cay – or Lignum Vitae Cay as it is properly named. He had just finished repairing the automatic lighthouse on nearby Great Stirrup Cay and was waiting for a flight home to Florida. I hated to tell him that I had spent the previous night in the anchorage behind Great Stirrup Cay and his lighthouse was definitely not working.)

However, hanging off the bowsprit with Mathew Wilson's cruising guide tucked under your arm is a good way of looking at the part of the bottom that the echo-sounder cannot reach. It can also help you decide if you are over the kind of ground that is going to securely embrace your anchor for the night.

Of course, none of this works if you can't see the bottom because the water is polluted or you are sailing through someone else's jetsam. But any sort of flotsam – plastic cola bottles, inflatable sun-beds, and far more disgusting artefacts – can tell you that land is nearby. That land might not be somewhere you particularly want to be, but if you are in a survival situation you don't really have much choice.

# PART THREE

# Do-it-Yourself Lo-Tech Navigation

THE HISTORY OF NAVIGATION is the history of the pursuit of accuracy. At the risk of being accused of attempting to turn the clock back, I have just taken you through a range of technology-free techniques for determining your *whereabouts* at sea. Now I am going to introduce some technology to make things a little more accurate.

'Why?' you might ask. If I am going to introduce technology at all, why can't I hand out GPS sets and be done with it? There are two reasons. Being able to improvise navigation aids and knowing how to use them will serve to reinforce your understanding of the fundamental rules of navigation. It also makes the knowledge imparted in this book more potentially useful in survival situations.

# Dead Reckoning

DEAD RECKONING is a simple means of estimating a position by applying course steered (specifically *assumed* course made good) and distance sailed (speed x time) from a last-known position. The expression is derived from '*deduced* reckoning', which is worth remembering because it does not sound nearly as accurate as 'dead reckoning'! This caution is especially apt when barefoot navigating because the chances are that the 'last-known position' was derived from a 'previously known position' using dead reckoning. In other words, any new errors could be compounding old errors.

In Part 2 we looked at different means of determining and holding a heading. So you know the approximate course you have been making good, but how far are you along that course? To determine that, you need to know the speed your boat has been making through the water, as well as the time travelled on that leg. In Part 3 we will look at methods for calculating your speed. Unless you have a watch, your time estimates are going to be in days or, at least, big fractions of a day. Thus all we need to do this calculation is:

> distance travelled = speed x time travelled

In most barefoot navigation – especially the survival kind – you will be working to fulfil a long-term strategy: 'I'm going to head due south to 13° and turn west, keeping slightly north of the latitude for ten days until the jets taking off and landing at Grantley Adams International Airport tell me I've reached Barbados.' Or more starkly, 'I want to get to the nearest coastline and get off this leaky tub!' Subtle course changes will be rare, and probably irrelevant, because they presume a confidence in your position that is not justified by the navigation techniques you are employing.

This straightforward approach might be imposed on you by the fact that you are having to hold the course in your head; you have no chart! The 'global position emergency locator' in Appendix 10 is designed to help you get a feeling for where you might be and what your options are for reaching a safe haven. This is best used in conjunction with the charts showing world ocean currents (Appendix 12) and prevailing wind systems (Part 2). Hopefully you copied these, or printed them from the website, and laminated them before tucking them away in your survival 'grab-bag'. The other possibility is to have the Admiralty pilot chart for the regions in which you are sailing; these show the prevailing wind directions and speeds and are the right kind of scale for survival situations.

There is another practical problem. A major cause of error in dead reckoning is the navigator's failure to make correct allowance for the extent to which surface currents, tide streams and the wind are conspiring to push the boat off the desired course. If you have been formally trained you will work out a course to steer by drawing the relevant vectors[49] on the chart. If you don't have a chart it is possible to make these calculations on a plain piece of paper as long as you have a straight-edge (preferably a ruler), a pencil, a protractor and, of course, a sheet of paper. If you lost all those, or you are trying to work without them as the ancient navigators did, then you are going to have to make the adjustments in your head.

What follows are rudimentary methods of calculating a position by dead reckoning; later we will consider how you might be able to make slightly more accurate estimates of latitude and longitude.

## IMPROVISING A COMPASS

No compass? This is unlikely to happen on board the boat itself, but it could occur in a survival predicament on a liferaft, deserted island or isolated coastline. These are the steps to follow if you need to improvise your own compass:

- *Locate a short length of wire, a sewing needle or, at a pinch, a pin.* A needle is best, but whatever you choose needs to have high ferrous (iron) content.
- *Now magnetise the needle.* There are a number of ways of doing this. If you have a magnet, use it to stroke the needle repeatedly, always in the same direction, until it is able to attract/repel other metal objects. (If you are still on a boat, you might be able to find a magnet inside unusable electrical gear. Start with one of the speakers from the hi-fi system. You will also find magnets in the engine starter motor and alternators.) The second technique involves the use of a battery or batteries with a potential in excess of 3 volts. Using *insulated* wire, fashion a coil around the needle (the more coils the better) and connect the ends to the positive and negative terminals. Leave for 5 to 10 minutes. Finally, although I've never tried this, some magnetism can be induced into the needle by stroking it with a piece of silk cloth. (You may need a volunteer with silk underwear for this.)

❋ *Now you have to suspend the needle in some way.* A piece of *untwisted* thread tied around the centre will serve. If you have a well-magnetised needle, one that snaps reasonably sharply to north, it is better to use a glass jar or plastic beaker partially filled with water (see Fig 3.1). The needle can be suspended on a sliver of balsa wood, a slip of paper or, if you are ashore, a piece of leaf or seaweed.

❋ *Calibration comes next.* Make sure you know which end of the needle is pointing north. The sun or stars will help you do this. If you have the needle floating in a container, you might be able to mark it up (using a Chinagraph pencil or pieces of adhesive tape) with a crude compass card. If you can do better than eight divisions (north, north-east, east, etc), then you are doing very well. A light line or wire stretched tightly between north and south on your improvised card might well prove helpful to the helmsman should you be able to get under way.

I understand that it is possible to magnetise a razor blade by stropping it against the palm of the hand then suspending it vertically. (Don't try this in rough seas and without the supervision of a trauma surgeon!) Whatever device you use, remember to top up the magnetism every few days, at least. Also remember that the needle will be pointing towards *magnetic* north. The variation from true north will depend on where you are in the world and may well be the least of your worries.

Some metal objects seem to hold a little magnetism, maybe enough to provide a rough indication of north. Take the pull-ring or lid from a soft-drink can or the lid from a can of baked beans, clean it up, flatten it, and float it in a tumbler of water. Now watch it for a while. Does it settle in a particular direction? Move it and see if it happens again and it rotates to the same place? Mark the lid in some way. You shouldn't have too much trouble in determining whether it is pointing north or south and it should be pointing to both.

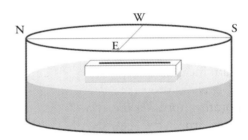

**Fig 3.1** Floating needle compass.

# THE WATCH COMPASS

You may have learned this trick as a Scout, a Pioneer or whatever: but if I'm going to allow the 21st century barefoot navigator a watch, then we may as well find some extracurricular uses for it – but it has to be a proper watch, one with hands!

A few cautionary notes to begin with:

1  The watch must be set to unadjusted local time net of daylight saving.
2  The lower the latitude, the lower the accuracy.
3  You need an analogue watch – the type with a big hand and a little hand and numbers that go around the outside of the dial.

Also, a slightly different method is used for finding south in the southern hemisphere.

In the northern hemisphere, hold the watch horizontally. Point the hour hand towards the sun. A line bisecting the angle between the hour hand and 12 o'clock now points to true north (see Fig 3.2).

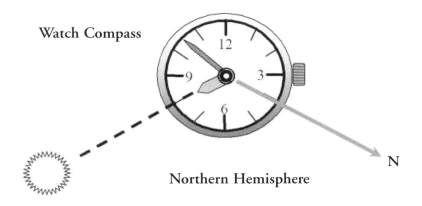

**Fig 3.2** Finding north with a watch.

In the above example, it is just before 8 am local time. The watch is being held in such a way that the hour hand is pointing towards the sun. A line extending from the centre of the watch through the mark for four o'clock points in the direction of north.

In the southern hemisphere, hold the watch, keeping the face horizontal. Point the number 12 towards the sun. A line bisecting the angle between the hour hand and 12 now points south (see Fig 3.3). In the example, it is just before eight o'clock again, the number 12 is pointing towards the sun, and the direction of south is indicated by a line bisecting the 4 (halfway between 12 and 8).

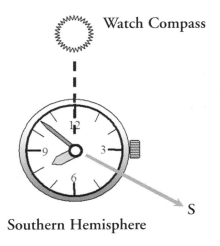

**Fig 3.3** Finding south with a watch.

To reassure yourself that this does actually work, get up early and try it at dawn. Assuming this is at six o'clock and you are pointing the hour hand (on number 6) at the sun, you will be looking towards the east, and north will be square off to your left (halfway between the direction of the sun and the number 12). The same check applies in the antipodes, but for south.

This is slightly more accurate than just kind of knowing the time, eyeballing the sun, and waving your arm in the right general direction – but not a lot more. As an indication of how far technology has gone, I recently found myself wearing a Suunto *digital* watch which, at the touch of a button, became a wrist compass. With in-built barometer and altimeter, it was more James Bond than Baden-Powell. While playing with this (it came with an instruction manual the size of *Yellow Pages*) a thought occurred to me: why do the hands on a clock go round? Why don't they go up and down or in and out? The rotation is significant in some way. It could be that early clockmakers found it easier to release the energy of a coiled spring by using precisely engineered cogs and gear-wheels. Everything goes round in one direction or another and at different speeds until the minute hand and hour hand are presented to the user of the watch – one rotating once every hour, the other once every day.

If this is essentially expedient, it is also fortuitous. Essentially we measure time by the rotation of the Earth. We perceive that rotation by seeing how the celestial sphere appears to rotate around the Earth. We will come back to this when we look at a really impressive way of estimating our *longitude* from the rotation of the stars.

## THE DUTCHMAN'S LOG

This is probably the lowest of low-tech solutions to a navigation problem. If all the high tech has failed, here's how to make a rough guess of your speed:

- Preparation: mark off a distance of 25ft (7.62m) along one side of your boat. You might get lucky with the stanchions – otherwise stick on some tape.
- Toss a small floating object into the water ahead of the forward mark and not too far from the hull. (Try to avoid the bow wake which will send it off at an angle.) A small piece of wood, an un-needed cat or an unruly child will do. (Only kidding – I wouldn't do that to a cat.)
- Check the time it takes for the object to pass by the measured 25ft. Use a stop-watch if you have one. Counting 'one thousand and two thousand…' is barely accurate enough. Let's assume that the object whizzes by in 3 seconds.
- Multiply that by 100: 3 x 100 = 300. Then multiply the number of feet measured off (25) by 60: 25 x 60 = 1,500. Divide the result of that by 300: 1,500/300 = 5 *knots*. This is the perfect round number of ocean cruising; it gives you 120nm per day which, as they say, is sufficient.

To save you from the mental arithmetic, Table 3.1 shows the speeds corresponding to each second the log takes to pass 25ft – which is 7.62m.

| MEASURE | TIME | SPEED IN KNOTS |
|---------|------|----------------|
| 25ft/7.62m | 1s | 15.00 |
| 25ft/7.62m | 2s | 7.50 |
| 25ft/7.62m | 3s | 5.00 |
| 25ft/7.62m | 4s | 3.75 |
| 25ft/7.62m | 5s | 3.00 |
| 25ft/7.62m | 6s | 2.50 |
| 25ft/7.62m | 7s | 2.14 |
| 25ft/7.62m | 8s | 1.88 |

**Table 3.1**

# THE HOME-BREW LOG-SHIP

Here is another type of *log* you can improvise. The design is based on the traditional device called a log-ship.

Take a heavy piece of marine plywood (5-ply or more) and cut it into an equilateral triangle with sides of about 30cm (see Fig 3.4). Drill a small hole in the top and bottom left corners of the board. Drill a bigger hole of about 0.5cm in the bottom right corner. Sand down the edges and varnish (if you want to keep it for future emergencies).

Along the bottom edge fold a strip of lead and pin it in place. If you don't have any lead on board, attach some heavy bolts (the ones that the chandler promised were marine stainless steel, but are now rusted to hell and back). This is to keep the board upright.

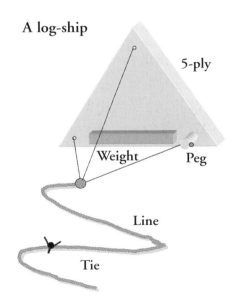

**A log-ship**

5-ply

Weight    Peg

Line

Tie

**Fig 3.4** An improvised log-ship.

Fashion three lengths of braided fishing line and secure the ends together. Pass one end through the top hole (the one opposite the weight) and tie the end in a figure-of-eight knot. Do the same with the bottom hole.

Fashion a wooden peg so that it fits firmly into the other bottom hole and secure the third line to the end of that. Make sure that the three lines are of equal length; this is particularly important if you want to use the log more than once. As you deploy the log, all the pressure on it goes to pulling the line out. Once you tug on the line, there needs to be enough pressure on the peg to jerk it out of the hole. This will make the board go flat so that you can haul it in.

Tie the above arrangement to a long length of similar braided line, ideally non-stretch or pre-stretched. (If you already have a braided fishing line on board, use that.)

Now put marks on the line. These can be knots or ribbons of cloth; you can even use colourful plastic cable ties pulled really tight. Fix them at intervals of 14.4m (47ft 3in) from the face of the board.

The log is used like this. Making sure the line will run out freely, throw the log over the stern. As the first knot goes out, check the second hand on your watch or, if you have one, start your stop watch. Count the number of knots that go out in exactly 28 seconds. That is your speeds – in knots! If you want to improve the accuracy, mark half-intervals with a different colour ribbon. When the 28 seconds is up, tug the line and the peg should pop out. This flattens the board so you can pull it back in. Obviously, the above process will need to be repeated whenever wind conditions change. (If you were wondering how they managed to time 28 seconds in the days before accurate ship's chronometers, they used hour glasses which contained exactly 28 seconds of sand.)

Now you have an estimate of your speed, and from that you can calculate your distance made good. Combined with the course you have been trying to hold, you should be able to get a rough-and-ready dead reckoning position. This can be cross-checked against an estimate of your boat's latitude.

# Latitude

## KAMALS AND POLAR STICKS

THE VIKINGS travelled along 61°N from Norway to Iceland and Greenland so often that it was probably worth their while marking the latitude of Polaris on their mast, thus turning it into the ultimate 'polar stick'. It does, however, lack versatility.

Fig 3.5 shows a simple polar stick calibrated in degrees of latitude. You should not, of course, copy these calibrations because the distance between the marks relate to the length of your arm – the distance between your eye and the stick. Each barefoot navigator will have to make his own 'instrument' from a boat (or a north-facing shore), the latitude of which he can be reasonably certain about. The Vikings probably did this from a longship being navigated by a mentor with a well-proved stick.

The marks can be notches that you can feel with your fingernail. If you insist on being a little hi-tech, then luminous paint will do the job. Plastic rulers and the edges of a Breton Plotter can also serve as polar sticks. You need to be able to see a reasonably clear horizon and make sure that you are measuring the altitude of Polaris and not the brightest star in the general direction of north. You should be aiming at an accuracy of 1°; this is not enough for pilotage of course, but at least you don't need batteries.

The *kamal* used by the Arabs works on the same principle, but the use of the knotted line held between the teeth was an alternative

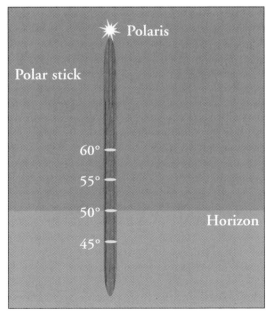

**Fig 3.5** A polar stick.

to calibrating the edges of the device. It is probably possible to use a combination of both; the knot gives you the nearest 10°, the marks on the board itself being calibrated in single degrees.

The polar stick strikes me as being simpler to implement, but I have to confess to having affection for the kamal. I have won a number of bets by telling sailors that I could determine a latitude by using a hand-held GPS receiver without the batteries. We would all tramp out onto the deck (or onto the dock if in the marina bar) and I would then use my own GPS as a kamal to check the elevation of the Pole Star. It has to be my little Magellan because I know how its dimensions translate into degrees of altitude. (I have already checked that I will be able to see both Polaris and the horizon.) It's a little street magic that is worth a free drink!

## THE ASTROLABE, THE CROSS-STAFF AND THE BACKSTAFF

As was made clear in Part 1, the astrolabe was originally designed as an instrument for astronomers and the metres-high versions built for observatories were impractical for use on a ship at sea. Later metal versions were more compact, more portable and almost certainly were used by Arab navigators crossing deserts and oceans. Although it was far too fancy a device to be worth replicating for practical use, it did have an arm and a calibrated scale that could be used for measuring elevations; that much we can learn from.

Early in the Age of Exploration the indispensable tool of the navigator was the 'cross-staff'. Also known as the 'fore-staff', the cross-staff was an early, rudimentary instrument used for measuring the altitude of celestial objects such as the sun, moon and stars. The device consisted of a cross-bar that slides along a calibrated wooden staff. The observer held the end of the staff to his upper cheek and then positioned the cross-bar so that the top of the bar touched the object at the same time that the bottom touched the horizon. The altitude was then read off the calibrations on the staff. Being versatile, cheap and relatively easy to use, the cross-staff was the navigator's instrument of choice for centuries. The downside was that, even with the use of smoked glass shades, the use of this device over a period of time caused blindness, the occupational hazard for navigators at that time.

A solution was found in the 'backstaff', a navigation instrument that dated from Renaissance times, but was still in use in the 18th century; while measuring the altitude of the noon sun, the observer would have his back to the sun. It functioned by casting a shadow from the end of a sliding *upper index* onto a *horizon vane*. The vane included a narrow horizontal slot which could be sighted through a pin-hole at the end of a sliding *lower index*. The upper index is calibrated for 60°, the lower index for 30°. The observer pre-sets the upper index to an estimated value and then moves the lower index until he can see the edge of the shadow level with the horizon as seen through the slot in the vane. He then adds the setting of the two indexes to obtain the altitude.

Sadly, though, the backstaff lacked the versatility of the cross-staff because it was useless in sighting stars. The device was first described by Captain John Davis in his 1585 book *The Seaman's Secrets* and was often referred to as 'the Davis quadrant'.

## IMPROVISING QUADRANTS

I described in Part 1 how our hands can be used to make a rough and ready measurement of angles. Such techniques can be used to estimate our latitude. By improvising an instrument called a quadrant, we can make those measurements considerably more accurate. Why not a sextant? For the simple reason that a sextant requires optics that are nigh on impossible to make yourself and certainly couldn't be improvised in a survival situation.

Using the skies to determine a position is all about measuring angles, specifically the vertical angle between the horizon and a specific celestial object. This angle is called the *altitude* of the sun or star because it's a way of determining the height of the object above the horizon. At school we are all taught to measure angles using a semi-circular piece of plastic called a *protractor*. Angles from zero to 180º are marked off along the semi-circular edge of the protractor; you will remember using one of these when learning geometry. If you can find your old school protractor, do what I did – transfer it to your on-board survival kit. You could always try begging a spare one from your offspring.

Converting the protractor into an improvised quadrant is a relatively simple matter, but please read all these instructions before you start! First of all, you need to put your hands on a reasonably long piece of wood (50cm or about 18in) that has a straight edge. This you will use for 'sighting'. Next, find a way of attaching the protractor to the sighting board. General-purpose glue, if you have such a thing, will do the job. Alternatively, find a couple of small nails. Do not drive these through the plastic because you will shatter it. Protractors usually have a hole in the middle; drive the nails in here at an angle so that the protractor is held firmly in place. *It is essential to ensure that the straight edge of the protractor is parallel to the straight edge of the sighting board* (see Fig 3.6). Moving the angled nails will help you to make fine adjustments.

Finally, you need to find a way of fixing a length of line to the centre of the protractor; this will be the 'plumb line' or 'plumb bob' – 'plumb' being from the Latin for 'lead'. You need this because, without the kind of optics you get in a sextant, you have no way of relating the celestial body to the horizon. But a vertical line where you are standing goes right up to your zenith *and is at right*

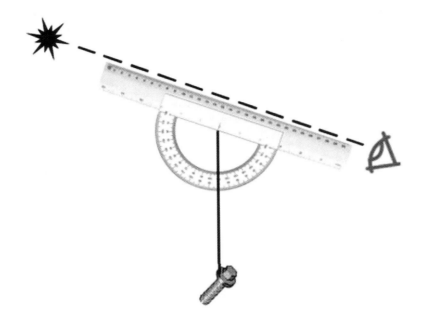

**Fig 3.6** An improvised quadrant using a protractor.

*angles to the horizon.* This is even better than using the horizon because you are no longer dependent on its visibility at night or in unhelpful weather conditions.

Light mono-filament fishing line is perfect for the job and you should have some of this in your survival kit. There should already be a hole at the centre of the protractor's base line which is normally used to centre the instrument on the apex of the angle to be measured. With a little luck, you might have a pin or very small nail which you can drive through this hole – again, be careful not to break the protractor. The end of the line can then be tied to the pin. If you don't have a pin, thread the line through the hole and secure it to the reverse of the protractor with a little adhesive. If you don't have any adhesive, tie a figure-of-eight knot in the end and carve a little hollow in the side of the sighting board so that the protractor still sits flat. (You need to do this *before* attaching the protractor to the board, which is why I warned you to read all the instructions before starting...) Now attach a weight to the other end of the line to keep it straight.

Finally, your quadrant can be improved even further by using a rigid arm instead of fishing line for reading off the scale. A thin piece of aluminium or plastic will do the job fine, but you still need to add weight to the lower end and the upper end needs to be bolted through the board at the axis of the scale. The whole thing needs to swing freely of course.

To 'calibrate' your new angle-measurer, point it at the horizon, taking care to get the back end of the sighting board in line with the front end and in line with the horizon. If you don't have someone with you to 'read' the point at which the plumb line crosses the edge of the protractor, you will have to press the line to the protractor and hold it there with a thumb or finger so you can read it yourself. It must, of course, say 90º. If it says 91º, for example, then the straight edge of the protractor is not perfectly aligned with the edge of the sighting board. Don't try and fix this problem; allow for the discrepancy when you take a sighting.

You should be trying to achieve accuracy to the nearest 1° at the very least. If you have the time, practise to get better and better altitudes. And if you are planning a long trip with youngsters on board, this is a great project with which to get them interested in navigation. Remind them *not* to point it at the sun, of course.

The fundamental problem with our rudimentary quadrant is that its accuracy is limited by the size of the protractor. To make something bigger we need a piece of wood; a 15cm square piece of marine 5-ply would be fine, 20cm square even better. We also need to make some sights, but let's deal with the problem of the scale first.

The scale needs to run from 0º to 90º and one way of doing it would be to draw it directly onto one side of our 5-ply board using our protractor and a ruler. If you are not confident about doing this straight onto the surface of the wood, draw it onto a sheet of tracing paper. Then shade over the lines on the reverse of the paper using a soft pencil. Fix the tracing paper firmly to the side of the board and draw over the lines again so that a 'trace' of the lines is left on the wood. Go over these using a ball-point pen to make the impression reasonably permanent. Another technique is to draw the scale on a sheet of regular paper and then carefully glue the paper to the wood. Obviously, that is unlikely to be permanent in wet weather, so you will need to give it a few coats of clear varnish (see Fig 3.7).

An alternative way of originating the scale is to use a drawing program on a personal computer. If you don't have a suitable program for doing this you will find one I made earlier on my website at jack-lagan.com. It is in a common computer graphics format. Just print it out, then you can laminate, trace or stick as you prefer.

Now let's get really pessimistic; you don't have a protractor with you and you didn't put a copy of my quadrant scale in your navigator's survival kit. But you might have a compass rose somewhere, maybe on a spare chart, maybe from a plotting chart (which usually come in pads). They look something like the one shown in Fig 3.8.

Cut out the rose and stick it to a flat piece of board. (If you can't find the adhesive, do you have a stapler on board? That might do the trick.) In this case, you don't need to worry about getting a good alignment with the edge of the board.

To improve the accuracy of your new quadrant you need to devise a set of 'gun sites' to be fitted on the top edge of the instrument. My preferred approach is to acquire two short pieces of plastic tube. The eye piece (at the rear) needs to be about 1cm *internal* diameter. The front site needs to be about 1cm *external* diameter. By aligning the fore sight in the rear sight, you are holding the board straight. Then you are ready to aim it at the target star, always checking that the

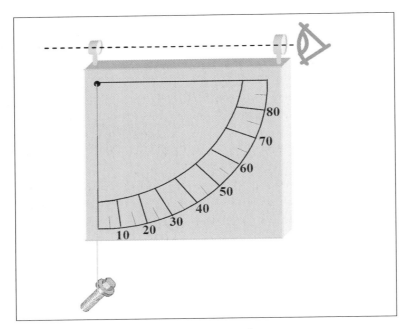

**Fig 3.7** A basic quadrant.

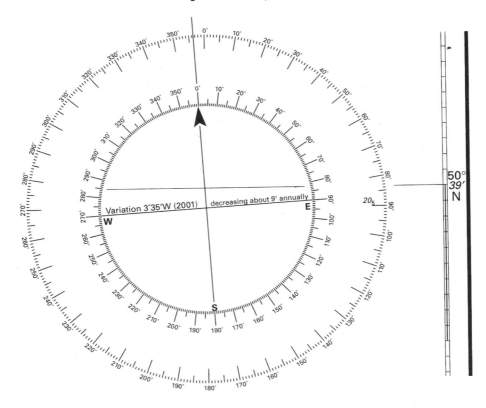

**Fig 3.8** A chart compass rose.

sights are still in line of course. The weighted line will provide the reading for the altitude. The reading of the altitude will be more precise because the scale is far bigger than using a protractor; now a real barefoot navigator will be looking for accuracy of 0.25º.

**Don't take sights of the sun by looking directly through the improvised sights.**

A modification to your quadrant is needed for getting the altitude of the sun. Learning from history, we are going to make the same change that was made when the cross-staff was replaced by the backstaff; we will use the shadow of the sun. The modification is relatively simple. At the point at which we have fixed our plumb-bob (or swinging index arm) we need to add a gnomon, a shadow-stick. The stick needs to be 3cm or 4cm in length and not too thick. I use a wooden cocktail stick; these are usually quite hard and have a useful pointed end which can go into the hole from which the plumb-bob swings. The trick is that the gnomon needs to be square to the surface scale of the quadrant. It is very easy for it to be knocked out of true so I remove it afterwards using the quadrant and then, with some ritual, re-insert it and re-align it each time before use. Now you don't need to look at the sun at all, but stand square-on to it, getting the shadow sharp, its edges parallel and reading where it intersects with the scale. This is a much preferred solution when working singlehanded and the quadrant can still be used to sight stars directly through the sights.

## LATITUDE USING THE SUN AT NOON

Now it is time to put your new quadrant to work. In Part 2 we looked at how useful a reasonable latitude can be in ocean navigation. Of course, the more accurate that latitude is, the more useful it will be. With 21st century barefoot navigation I think we will allow ourselves a little of our own special knowledge and use the stars (below) and the sun to get a more precise calculation of our latitude.

We are already familiar with the use of the word *altitude* to mean the apparent height of the sun above the horizon expressed in terms of the number of degrees subtended at the point on the surface of the Earth from which you are making the measurement. We now need to introduce some terms that will already be familiar to those who have studied celestial navigation. First of all, our *zenith* is the point on the celestial sphere directly above our heads – in other words, 90º up from the horizon. The *zenith distance* (ZD) (see general schematic in Fig 3.9) is the number of degrees between the sun and our zenith. We don't need to measure this; if we subtract the altitude of the sun from 90º, then we will have the zenith distance. For example, if we measure an altitude of 50º, then the zenith distance must be 40º (90º – 50º = 40º).

If the sun is not exactly overhead and we can see it above the horizon, then the altitude will be a positive value. If we subtract that from 90, then we will get a positive zenith distance. However, if the sun is to our north, then we have to treat the zenith distance as being *negative*. The purpose of this is to ensure that when we have performed our calculation the resulting latitude is plus or minus; this tells us if it is north or south respectively. This will become clearer when we look at some worked examples.

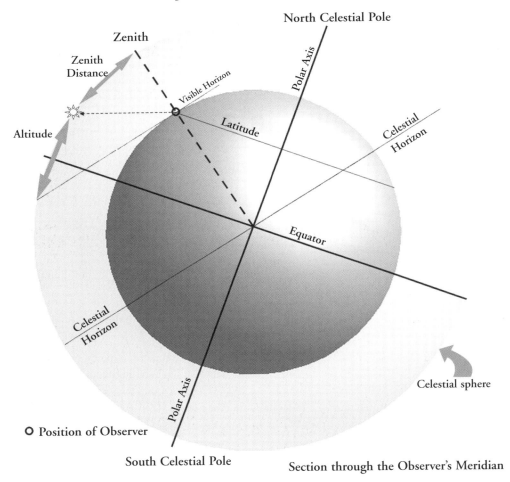

**Fig 3.9** Latitude from the altitude of a celestial body.

We need to add or subtract one further number to the zenith distance to get our latitude and that value is called the *declination* of the sun. We have come across this before when we considered the way in which the rising and setting points of the sun vary from 23.5°N to 23.5°S and back again throughout the year. (The exact figure is 23.45°, but barefoot navigators don't do one-hundredths of anything.) This cyclical change is caused by the fact that the Earth leans over by 23.5° and so, as it orbits the sun, it sometimes leans towards it and sometimes away. The declination is the amount of that 'lean' if you like.

The declination is different for each day of the year. This means that we need a table of all the possible values – and that's the 'special knowledge' we are inheriting.

Table 3.2 includes values that are accurate enough for 2006 and 2007. The declination doesn't change very much, so there are entries for intervals of four days only.

| JANUARY | | APRIL | | JULY | | OCTOBER | |
|---|---|---|---|---|---|---|---|
| 1 | −23.0 | 3 | 5.4 | 4 | 22.9 | 4 | −4.4 |
| 5 | −22.6 | 7 | 6.9 | 8 | 22.5 | 8 | −5.9 |
| 9 | −22.1 | 11 | 8.4 | 12 | 21.9 | 12 | −7.4 |
| 13 | −21.5 | 15 | 9.8 | 16 | 21.3 | 16 | −8.9 |
| 17 | −20.7 | 19 | 11.2 | 20 | 20.6 | 20 | −10.4 |
| 21 | −19.9 | 23 | 12.6 | 24 | 19.8 | 24 | −11.8 |
| 25 | −18.9 | 27 | 13.9 | 28 | 18.9 | 28 | −13.2 |
| 29 | −17.9 | | | | | | |

| FEBRUARY | | MAY | | AUGUST | | NOVEMBER | |
|---|---|---|---|---|---|---|---|
| 2 | −16.8 | 1 | 15.1 | 1 | 18.0 | 1 | −14.5 |
| 6 | −15.6 | 5 | 16.3 | 5 | 16.9 | 5 | −15.7 |
| 10 | −14.3 | 9 | 17.4 | 9 | 15.8 | 9 | −16.9 |
| 14 | −13.0 | 13 | 18.4 | 13 | 14.6 | 13 | −18.0 |
| 18 | −11.6 | 17 | 19.4 | 17 | 13.4 | 17 | −19.0 |
| 22 | −10.1 | 21 | 20.2 | 21 | 12.1 | 21 | −20.0 |
| 26 | −8.7 | 25 | 21.0 | 25 | 10.7 | 25 | −20.8 |
| | | 29 | 21.6 | 29 | 9.3 | 29 | −21.5 |

| MARCH | | JUNE | | SEPTEMBER | | DECEMBER | |
|---|---|---|---|---|---|---|---|
| 2 | −7.1 | 2 | 22.2 | 2 | 7.9 | 3 | −22.1 |
| 6 | −5.6 | 6 | 22.7 | 6 | 6.4 | 7 | −22.6 |
| 10 | −4.0 | 10 | 23.0 | 10 | 4.9 | 11 | −23.0 |
| 14 | −2.5 | 14 | 23.3 | 14 | 3.4 | 15 | −23.3 |
| 18 | −0.9 | 18 | 23.4 | 18 | 1.8 | 19 | −23.4 |
| 22 | 0.7 | 22 | 23.4 | 22 | 0.3 | 23 | −23.4 |
| 26 | 2.3 | 26 | 23.4 | 26 | −1.3 | 27 | −23.3 |
| 30 | 3.8 | 30 | 23.2 | 30 | −2.9 | 31 | −23.0 |

**Table 3.2** Declination of the sun for 2006 and 2007

To look up a declination, find the month and then go down the column below it to the nearest date. If you do not have any of the dates shown, you need to make an interpolation, or adjustment (you have a one-in-four chance of being right on the money). Let us assume that the date on which we are making the observation is 3 May. Look at Table 3.2 – the nearest entries are for 1 May, followed by 5 May. The declinations for those dates are +15.1º and +16.3º – a difference of 1.2º. Divide that by two and you get 0.6º, which is near enough for our purposes. Add that to +15.1º, giving +15.7º as the declination for 3 May. The '+' and '–' tells you whether the declination is north or south and, therefore, whether we need to add it to the zenith distance or subtract it.

Table 3.3 gives the four simple steps to estimate latitude when the sun is to your north (zenith distance is positive).

| | | |
|---|---|---|
| 1 | Use quadrant to read the altitude (alt) of the sun at local noon. | Example:<br>**alt = 65°** |
| 2 | Subtract altitude from 90° to obtain zenith distance. | ZD = 90° – alt<br>**ZD = 90° – 65° = 25°** |
| 3 | Use Table 3.2 (or Appendix 3) to obtain the declination of the sun for date of sight. | Date = 21 November<br>**Dec = –20°** |
| 4 | Add declination to zenith distance to obtain latitude. (Note: The sun is to the *north*, so zenith distance is negative.) | Lat = –ZD + Dec<br>Lat = –25° + (–20.0°) = –45.0°<br>**Or 45.0°S** |

**Table 3.3** Calculation of latitude when sun is north (zenith distance is positive).

Does 45ºS in Table 3.3 make sense? We are in the southern hemisphere in December – summer in that part of the world. You would expect the sun to be reasonably high in the sky and, at 65º, it is. Table 3.4 gives the four steps again. This time they are used to estimate latitude when the sun is to your south (zenith distance negative).

| | | |
|---|---|---|
| 1 | Use quadrant to read the altitude (alt) of the sun at local noon. | Example:<br>**alt = 50°** |
| 2 | Subtract altitude from 90° to obtain zenith distance. The sun is to the *south*. | ZD = 90° – alt<br>**ZD = 90° – 50° = +40°** |
| 3 | Use Table 3.2 (or Appendix 3) to obtain the declination of the sun for date of sight. | Date = 3 May<br>**Dec = +15.7°** |
| 4 | Add declination to zenith distance to obtain latitude. (Note: The sun is to the *south*, so zenith distance is positive.) | Lat = ZD + Dec<br>Lat = +40° + (+15.7°) = +55.7°<br>**Or 55.7°N** |

**Table 3.4** Calculation of latitude when sun is south (zenith distance is negative).

How accurate do you think 55.7º in Table 3.4 is going to be? I avoided putting more than one decimal place in Table 3.2 because I didn't want to mislead you about the likely precision of the result. The controlling factor is the altitude as read by you in a Force 5 on a small boat using your improvised quadrant. Using something like a small school protractor you won't do much better than 1° – 60nm. With a larger quadrant and a printed scale, you should try to get ¼° – 15nm. Not much good for port pilotage, but at least it tells you where you are not. As a navigator called Lecky put it, 'There is nothing so distressing as running on shore, unless there is also present some doubt as to which continent the shore belongs.'

The sun declination table in Appendix 3 is also shown in a reduced version in Appendix 4. The idea of the smaller copy is that you can photocopy it, laminate it, and keep it in your survival kit or stick it to the reverse of your quadrant. Both versions can be downloaded from the barefoot navigator website at jack-lagan.com. The table changes only slightly year-on-year so this one is good for 2006 and 2007. The year 2008 is a leap year and that disrupts the calendar, so I'll produce a new one before then.

## LATITUDE USING THE STARS

It is worth considering *why* the noon sun-shot is such a relatively straightforward way of obtaining the latitude of your position. (Although without a sextant it is much less accurate than working with the meridian-passage of stars.) We have already mentioned the concept of the *meridian*. Your meridian is a line that runs from the North Pole through your zenith (directly overhead) and on to the South Pole. When the sun is at its highest altitude of the day, local noon, it is right on your meridian. This simple consideration means that you do not have to get involved in tricky spherical geometry.

Keeping it simple by keeping it on the meridian is a very barefoot concept, and the good news is that it applies to the stars as well as the sun; now you can check your latitude more frequently. This does not mean that you are likely to be moving very quickly, but if the sun was obscured around local noon it might have been some time since you last checked. If your course strategy is based on chasing a latitude and you have a cross-current to deal with, you will become more than a little preoccupied with staying glued to your chosen track.

The principle of working with a star is the same as using the sun. Let's assume we have a good clear night; Mintaka in the constellation of Orion helped us to verify our course and it can help us with our latitude too. The procedure for monitoring its progress towards your meridian is the same as for the sun. Periodically check the altitude of the object with your quadrant. As the increase in altitude slows down, increase the frequency of checks until it seems it is not increasing any more. You should be making notes of the altitude at this point, if you can. The first time the altitude *decreases*, you know you have the reading for your meridian.

Now here comes the arithmetic. If Mintaka is to the south of you, subtract the altitude from 90° and you have your latitude. In other words, an altitude of 55° tells you that you are on latitude 35° N. If Mintaka is in the sky to your north, then you are at 35° S. (I just changed the sign of the zenith distance from plus to minus!) No, I didn't forget to allow for the declination – that only applies to the sun; consider it a huge bonus for working with stars. If you can't see Mintaka, you can use this procedure with any other bright star that looks as though it's going to be easy to see as it crosses your meridian. *However*, when you are in northern latitudes you must use southern stars and vice versa – below the Equator, choose a northern star.

There is another way of using the stars for the latitude that doesn't involve the use of the quadrant. You may recall that the angle at which stars rise above the horizon depends on the latitude of the observer. Fig 2.18 showed Orion rising when seen from 40°S; the angle its course makes with the horizon is 40°. The implication of this is that if you can measure this angle, then you have a ready-made latitude. Sadly, though, an accurate reading of the angle is only possible once the star has risen a reasonable distance from the horizon... and by then you will have a problem identifying the point at which it emerged.

## MAKING A SUN-SHADOW BOARD

I described in Part 1 how I thought Viking navigators could have made a sun-shadow board and how it might be used for staying on the desired latitude when crossing the northern reaches of the Atlantic Ocean between Norway, Iceland, Greenland and Vinland. These devices were also used by the Arabs for finding their way across deserts. They were used as recently as the Second World War when British Special Forces units operating in North Africa fitted them to their trucks and jeeps.[50]

Appendix 5 shows a schematic for a sun-shadow board you could make your-self. You need a piece of wood that is about 1.5cm thick and from which you can cut a circle about 8cm in diameter. The wood needs to be light in colour so that the markings and the shadow are as clear as possible; should that be a problem you might have to consider painting the 'face' with waterproof white paint. The top of the board must be dead flat and you can, and should, check that using a straight-edged ruler held across it at a variety of angles.

Once you have prepared the board, use a pair of drawing compasses to inscribe a series of circles as shown in Appendix 5. These need to be as accurate as you can make them. Next to each one write the latitude to which it refers.

Alternatively, make a copy of the template included in Appendix 5 or download it from the website at jack-lagan.com and print it out. In both cases, double-check that accuracy has not been lost *en route* to hard copy. Then you can glue the print-out to the top of the board and apply a couple of coats of clear varnish to protect it from the weather and the sea.

Next you need to make the gnomon, the shadow-pointer. This must be 7cm in length, no more than the thickness of a pencil and pointed at the top. Now comes the chore of marking the side of the gnomon every 1mm from the top for 55mm. To make it easier to read, inscribe a longer mark at each centimetre. The best way to make the marks is by using a scalpel or sharp knife, carefully cutting thin notches into the wood. This is to prevent the marks being erased whenever you adjust the height of the gnomon in the hole you now need to drill right in the centre of the disc – at the exact point from which you measured the radius of the circles. The hole needs to be pretty much a perfect fit for the gnomon; big enough for you to be able to adjust the gnomon to the nearest millimetre mark, tight enough to keep it in place when you use the board.

The next item is a luxury feature. A common complaint about the sun-shadow board is the need to keep the top surface as horizontal as possible. Let's rule out beer bottles and buckets of water and go for a small spirit level, the type that holds the liquid in a bubble of glass or clear plastic. These can be found in most DIY chain stores. Drill a recess into the top surface of the disc so that it will fit snugly. Place the disc on a flat work-surface and check that it is *absolutely* level (maybe using a carpenter's spirit level). If the top and bottom surfaces are not parallel, slip pieces of paper under the edge of the disc until the top surface is horizontal; it is the top surface that is important here. Now drop a little glue into the recess and press the spirit bubble into place, making certain the bubble of air sits squarely inside the ring marked on the top of the glass.

The handle underneath the board needs to be hollow so that you have a means of pushing the gnomon upwards if it gets a little stuck. The best solution for this is probably a length of plastic plumbing pipe with the right internal and external dimensions. It can be super-glued to the bottom of the board over the hole. A few coats of varnish will finish the whole thing off.

Finally, you need to know how to set the height of the gnomon for the day of the year. So that you don't need to sit on a draughty mountain overlooking a Norwegian fjord to do this, I have created a table and this is included as Appendix 6. Look up your date of departure and set the height of the gnomon to the number of millimetres shown. For example, if you are leaving on 16 July and planning to follow a latitude of 40ºN, then you need to set the gnomon to 45mm. Values are shown for every four days (to save space) but, if you are delayed by bad weather and are only able to leave on 18 July, then split the difference between the 16th and the 20th – 45mm and 43mm – and adjust the gnomon so it has a height of 44mm. The scale is in whole millimetres because I'm not confident that it's really possible to calibrate the gnomon any more accurately.

Take a look at the height setting for the anticipated length of your voyage and you will see that an adjustment may have to be made every day or so. For example, if you are leaving on 16 July and have an ETA of 5 August, you will need to remember to reduce the height of the gnomon by 2mm before you take each noon shadow reading. This adjustment varies according to the time of year, so you can leave the height at 8mm for the whole of December (if on latitude 40º). If you are going to follow a latitude for which there is no circle on the board, then you will have to guess the intermediate values. Note that the instrument is not very effective at latitudes less than 35º and more than 60º.

This device is far more complicated than anything the Vikings (or any other ancient seafarers) may have used, but that added complexity comes from increasing its geographical coverage. It is a lot more straightforward if you are only interested in one or two specific latitudes.

# Longitude

## THE UBIQUITOUS QUARTZ WATCH

IT SEEMS THAT LINES OF LATITUDE did not appear on charts until the Greek astronomer Claudius Ptolemy published his 'world atlas' in the second century CE. Ptolemy proposed that everything whizzed around the Earth and this either made him ultra-conservative in the grand scale of things or, if you wish, remarkably prescient in anticipating the essential navigation concept of the celestial sphere. Sitting in the Egyptian port of Alexandria working on the meticulous detail of his atlas – and no doubt cursing deadlines and budgets – Ptolemy never knew how fortunate he was that his world did not go far beyond the Mediterranean. Nevertheless, his maps did include both latitude *and longitude*. Perhaps he thought he would get around to solving the longitude problem by the time the atlas was published.

So, how about a little barefoot longitude to go with all that latitude you have been estimating? The only additional 'instrument' you are going to need for these methods is a reasonably good quartz watch set to Greenwich Mean Time (GMT) or, as it is now known, Universal Time (UT). You will sometimes see this written as 'UTC', which means Universal Time Corrected. From now on we will refer to 'UT' and, when I want to reinforce the point that it refers to the time at Greenwich in London, 'GMT'.

Latitude indicates where we are north or south of the Equator. Longitude tells us where we are east or west of the Greenwich meridian – an arbitrary circle that circumscribes the Earth passing through both Poles and the Greenwich Observatory on the south bank of the River Thames in London. It is there because the Brits were taking the lead on this longitude thing and obviously were not going to draw it through Paris or Madrid. Or Beijing, for that matter.

If you have read Dava Sobel's inspired and inspiring book *Longitude*[51] you will understand that longitude is all about time. To calculate a longitude anywhere in the world you need to know, as accurately as possible, the time at Greenwich. In the heady days of European exploration and voyaging most clocks were 'powered' by a pendulum. These were, of course, intended to be firmly fixed to a wall or to stand on the steady floor of a house; they were not designed to cope with the pitching and rolling of a ship at sea. In those days, a ship's pendulum chronometer set exactly to GMT in the Port of London would be inaccurate before the shore lines were on board.

The book *Longitude* tells the remarkable tale of a fine Yorkshire clock-maker called John Harrison (1693–1776). Harrison struggled for years to design and build a clock that would work on a ship and that would be accurate enough to be used to calculate longitude to half a degree anywhere on Earth. The reward for success was impressive; the British government was offering a prize of £25,000 – a king's ransom in those days. After decades of not quite getting it quite right, the determined Harrison eventually put up 'Chronometer Number 4' for testing. The clock was installed on a ship due to depart on a round trip to Jamaica. On its return it was found to be five seconds late; that is equivalent to 1.25 minutes of arc, well within the jackpot-winning target of 30 minutes of longitude.

John Harrison would have been much impressed with the quartz-crystal used to drive modern clocks and watches. These rarely vary in accuracy beyond plus or minus one second in *ten years*. The clocks themselves are, of course, much less accurate, but that is because of the variable quality of the engineering that converts the timing signal into pointing hands or numbers that the owner can read.

As a large percentage of the world's population has one of these strapped to their wrists, I will add it to the barefoot navigator's toolbox. The one I keep in my personal survival kit is a medium-priced Sekonda *Xposé*. A few years ago I was working in Bosnia and the Sekonda decided to stop. I was unable to find a shop where I could get the battery replaced, but I was able to bluff my way into a Norwegian PX (a store for military personnel and aid workers) and got a very good price on a new Casio. I later removed the straps from the Sekonda, set it to UT and tucked it away in my survival kit. Attached to the watch is a waterproof key fob that contains a piece of paper showing 'UT Error = +10s'. This does not mean that the watch isn't accurate, but that it is impossible to adjust the second hand.

Let's assume that you are about to set your watch to 0800 (8am) UT. You pull out the little button and twiddle it until the minute and hour hands are showing eight o'clock. But the second hand is not adjustable and, in my case, it pointed to ten seconds after the hour. (My new watch automatically resets the second hand to 12 when I pull the button out.) You are tuned to a broadcast radio station that does time checks and, as the last pip sounds, you push the button in and the watch starts working again – but it is ten seconds fast. Those ten seconds are fairly critical, so you need to make a note of this 'error'. You can use a piece of tape stuck to the back of the watch or, as I did, a key fob attached to one of the bars to which the strap used to be fixed.

The only thing you need to worry about now is the battery life. This can be anything between one and two years according to the watch, so also make a note of the date on which the battery was last replaced. I always travel with a spare battery and the tool jewellers use to remove the back from a watch. Whenever the battery is renewed, remember to reset the watch to GMT using a broadcast time signal.

Do not believe the propaganda. You cannot get a longitude at sea using Saturn's moons, 'comfort zones' or tortured dogs.[52]

## USING THE SUN AT NOON

Essentially, the difference in time between where you are and the time at Greenwich will provide you with your longitude. That is why you need the watch. Each hour of difference represents 15º of longitude measured east or west of the Greenwich meridian (because the Earth rotates about 360º in 24 hours and 360/24 = 15). Greenwich is the 0º meridian, of course.

The watch gives you the essential head start because all you have to do is look at it and, after making any adjustment for 'errors' associated with the second hand, you've got the time at Greenwich. What about local time? Clearly you need to time some event that happens at Greenwich and which, earlier or later, also happens where you and your boat are sitting. This is where the sun comes in. The sensible convention is to use the sun at noon. The most obvious reason for this is that 1200 (12pm) GMT was originally defined by the transit of the sun, when at its highest point, *across the Greenwich meridian*. (The less obvious reason is that you are already using local noon to determine your latitude.) When you look at your quartz watch and it reads noon, you know that the sun is transiting the Greenwich meridian at that very instant, more or less. Calculating your longitude, therefore, is based on you timing the sun (using the same GMT watch) passing through *your* north–south meridian.

Let's take an example using round numbers. You monitor the passage of the sun, waiting for it to reach its highest point and you note the time. The watch reads 1500 (3pm). So, three hours ago, the sun was above the Greenwich meridian. The Earth rotates at 15º per hour, which means that you are 3 x 15 = 45° *west* of Greenwich – somewhere in the middle of the Atlantic anywhere between Cape Farewell at the southern tip of Greenland and the Amazon basin. (At this stage you know the altitude of the sun, so you will be able to narrow things down with a latitude.)

Here is another example; at local noon your chronometer reads exactly 0400 (4am) placing you on 8 x 15 = 120° or longitude 120ºE. (If you are also on latitude 15ºS, this places you off the north-west coast of Australia.)

That probably seems painless enough, but there are some issues that need to be resolved. How do you know whether you are east or west of Greenwich? How do you deal with any 'error' in the watch? And how do you know *exactly* when the sun is crossing your meridian?

You are west of Greenwich if the time on the watch is greater than the equivalent time at the longitude of 0º. In the first example, 1500 is greater than 1200, so you are west. There is a handy *aide memoir*: 'Best is West'. In the second example, 0400 is less than 1200 and 'Least is East'.

If your watch is running 'fast' by ten seconds, noon GMT is actually when your watch reads ten seconds *before* 1200. On the Equator, 1º of longitude is 60nm and, therefore, one minute of arc is 1nm or 1,852m (6,076ft). Forget about the ten seconds and you are already 300m out of position! This barefoot method is not accurate enough for you to be able to overlook such a discrepancy.

In a perfect universe, the Earth would be dead upright, rotate precisely 360º in each 24 hours and circle the sun unerringly every 365 days (or, even better, some decimal value like 1,000). By now you should be used to the idea that the world is tilted and burps and twitches its way around the sun. Its course is not a circle but an ellipse and, as our Japanese quartz watch ticks on with admirable accuracy, our planet whizzes through space faster in summer than it does in winter. As a consequence of this 'unintelligent design' we have to make an adjustment that could be as much as 16º and is, therefore, far more significant than any error we might get from our second hand.

This difference between what our watch is doing and what the Earth is doing is called 'the Equation of Time' (EoT). This is shown as a table and a graph in Appendices 7 and 8; like the declination of the sun, it is one of the date-related variations that we need to keep in our personal survival kits. The tables for the declination of the sun and the Equation of Time look very similar – be careful not to confuse them. An important difference is that the declination varies slightly from year to year, whereas the EoT is perennial – it doesn't change. Another difference is that the declination is an *angle*, whereas the EoT is in minutes of *time*.

The table in Appendix 8 shows the numbers for every four days of the year; you will need to interpolate between the nearest values for intermediate dates. The graph in Appendix 7 plots those values, and from this you will be able to see that the changes follow an odd double-peaked curve. That is worth studying. An innovative navigator called Tony Crowley has even come up with a poem that might help, should you become separated from the graph or the table:

> 14 minutes late around St Valentine's Day,
> 4 minutes early in the middle of May,
> 6 minutes late near the end of July,
> 16 minutes early when Halloween's nigh.
> The differences last about two weeks,
> Around these pairs of troughs and peaks.

With a calendar or a diary, there is enough information there for you to be able to make a rough reconstitution of the graph. Note that 'early' means '+' and 'late' means '−'.

Now down to business. Timing the transit of the sun across your meridian is the most difficult – and crucial – part of this method and you need to concentrate on getting it right. Get out the quartz watch, pencil and paper and your back-staff or quadrant. (Don't look at the sun through the sights – use the gnomon.)

A few minutes before noon local time, you are going to start taking altitudes of the sun and timing them using GMT. You need to take a reading every 20 seconds and write it down, so this is a job best done double-handed, if sailing with a crew. Your helper calls out 'Mark!' at each 20 seconds and you call back the altitude. She writes this down next to the time. When you start, the numbers should increase. When they start to decrease, you can stop and perform the calculation. (Yes, this is the same process you used to work out your latitude, so you are going to get two co-ordinates for the price of one.) *To estimate your longitude you are looking for the Universal Time at which the altitude of the sun was at its greatest.* You already know how to calculate the latitude from the altitude.

Here is an example of the calculation you need to perform:

1  *Write down the time of local noon.* Let's assume that you get two altitudes of the sun that are the same, one at 16h 21m 40s and the other 20 seconds later at 16h 22m exactly. Split the difference so that your assumed Time of Solar Transit is 16h 21m 50s (GMT of course). Write that down. (See Table 3.5.)
2  Apply any watch error you might know about. In this case the watch is 20 seconds fast, so you need to subtract that to get a corrected time of Greenwich noon. You are working in seconds here, so it would be useful to convert to fractions of a minute: 16h 21m 30s becomes 16h 21.5m.
3  *Look up the Equation of Time* for the date of the sight, 5 May. In this case, you don't need to interpolate and the EoT is +3.3 minutes; add this to the corrected time of the transit, giving 16h 24.8m as the apparent solar time. The difference between that and 1200 (noon) is 4h 24.8m.
4  *Convert to degrees and minutes of longitude* – one hour = 15°, 4 minutes = 1° – and we get an estimated longitude of 66º 12m. Greenwich is 'best', so we add 'W' for west.

Now you can do the latitude using the method described earlier and, with care and practice, you will have a reasonable *estimated* position.

| Calculation of Longitude from Time of Local Noon on 5 May | |
| --- | --- |
| Time of Solar Transit | 16h 21m 50s |
| Watch error | –20s |
| Corrected time | 16h 21m 30s |
| | or 16h 21.5m |
| Equation of Time | +3.3m |
| Apparent Solar Time at Greenwich | 16h 24.8m |
| Local Solar Time | 12h 00.0m |
| Time difference | 4h 24.8m |
| Estimated longitude | **66° 12m W** |

Table 3.5

# USING A COMPASS

There is another particularly useful method of estimating noon sun; this involves the use of a magnetic compass. (You will still need your UT watch of course.) The transit of the sun across your meridian can be determined by finding its greatest altitude and we can use an 'altitude measurer' to do that, as described in the previous section. But when the sun is at its highest, it is also due south – at 180°. To determine that direction, we need a 'bearing measurer' – a compass, in other words. This is where a potential problem arises.

Most compasses are not happy about being angled up or down by more than a few degrees. There are hand-bearing compasses that incorporate a prism that enables you to 'bring down' the object (in this case, the sun) towards the horizon. If you do not have one of these, you will have to hope that your compass can be tilted enough to cope. In higher latitudes, the sun will probably be low enough in the sky for you to be able to manage with a conventional hand-bearing compass or even, in a survival situation, with a compass designed for use on land. This is no great tragedy because quadrants and backstaffs work better when the sun is arcing high across the sky and giving a more definite point of reversal. When the sun is low and flat-lining its way along the horizon, the compass comes into its own. As we will see, it can also be used when the sun is not visible at all at noon.

Some bridge compasses include a gnomon which casts a shadow across the scale whenever the sun is open for business. If the vessel is not pitching and rolling overmuch, this can be the easiest way of taking a bearing.

The principle involved is straightforward; you take timed bearings of the sun before and after noon, then use that to deduce the time of the transit. In practice it is recommended that you take a series of timed bearings and average these out. Here is how to go about it:

⚜ On a sheet of graph paper mark a range of bearings along the Y-axis (the vertical one).
⚜ Mark some intervals of time along the horizontal X-axis.
⚜ Plot the bearings by time as shown in Fig 3.10.

In our example, six bearings were timed over a period from 1147 to 1159. After all of these were plotted on the graph paper, a ruler was used to 'average' them. Where the line crosses the 180° line we have our local noon timed according to UT: 1151h 30s.

The next step is to perform the calculation for obtaining our longitude. It is the same method used when starting with an altitude and the example shows that on 11 April we are near 02° 30min E, somewhere in the North Sea (see Table 3.6).

Sadly, though, things are rarely quite that simple. Obviously we have allowed for the 'error' in our handy pocket chronometer. What we must also take account

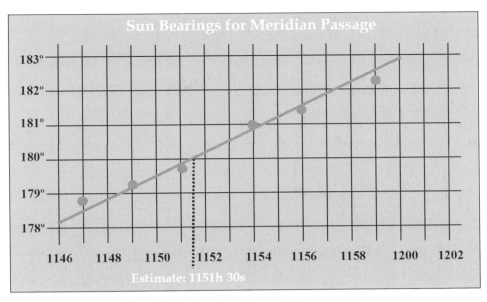

**Fig 3.10** Sun bearings for meridian passage.

of is any variation and deviation in the compass. Variation is the difference between true north and magnetic north; this varies according to where you are in the world. It also changes with time. Clearly, you need to have this information to hand but, even if you are adrift at sea, it is unlikely to have changed much since you said goodbye to your yacht. Deviation is a more serious irritation because it is caused by magnetic influence on the boat itself. If you are still on the boat, then you should have something called a 'deviation card' which tells you what adjustment to make for each point of the compass. You

| Calculation of Longitude from Time of Local Noon Sun | |
|---|---|
| Time of Solar Transit | 11h 51m 30s |
| Watch error | –18s |
| Corrected time | 11h 51m 12s |
| | or 11h 51.2m |
| EoT for 11 April | –1.2m |
| Apparent Solar Time at Greenwich | 11h 50.0m |
| Local Solar Time | 12h 00.0m |
| Time difference | 0h 10.0m |
| **Estimated longitude** (Greenwich is least) | **2° 30m E** |

**Table 3.6**

must try and get this resolved because it could adversely affect your bearing of the sun by as much as tens of degrees. Once you know the compass error it is a relatively simple matter to add it to, or subtract it from, 180° to get what is effectively a new meridian. For example, an error of –5° gives you a new meridian of 175° and you can read the time of the transit from that line on the graph.

The good news out of all this is that you do not need to be able to see the sun at local noon to get a longitude. Let's assume you have a miserable, cloudy day and it looks like you will not be able to update your estimated position for a while. Then, just before noon, the sun comes out and you grab your bearing compass and GMT watch. You manage to time two bearings (at 1147 and 1149 in Fig 3.11) before the cloud covers the sun again. Will it be enough? Two bearings are, of course, the minimum, but if you think they were reasonably accurate, plot them, draw an extended line through them and read your time of transit from that. Use every opportunity that you can; after all, the sun may appear again later in the afternoon and you will be able to draw a better graph using both sets of bearings.

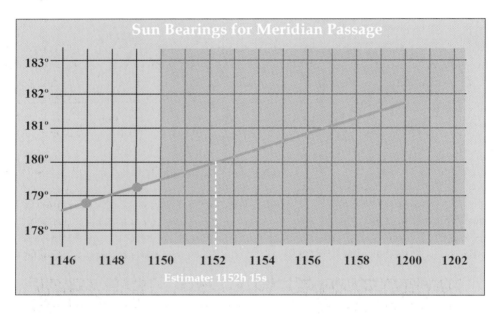

**Fig 3.11** Sun bearing for meridian passage (projection).

## LONGITUDE BY POLAR STICK

There is a third way of obtaining a rough longitude and it does not involve the use of compass, quadrant or backstaff – but you will still need the quartz watch set to GMT and the table, graph or poem for the Equation of Time (EoT).

This method relies on the fact that the sun rises and sets on the same latitude each day. You need your polar stick (if you made one) or a piece of wood or a knotted length of line. In the morning, as the sun is climbing into the sky, use your simple 'instrument' to determine when it has reached an easy-to-check altitude. Note the time at Greenwich. As the sun begins to descend, keep checking its altitude until it has reached the *same* height as your morning sight. Note the time again. Subtract the morning time from the afternoon time, halve it, and add it to the morning time. Now you have a rough estimate of the time the sun transited your meridian. Apply the EoT for the date of the sight, subtract the result from 12 hours, and convert to degrees and minutes of arc to obtain your approximate longitude.

This is probably the crudest of methods but, done with care, might be critically helpful in a survival situation. If it is not the crudest of methods, then the one that uses the star Kochab might be.

## A MINIMALIST LONGITUDE USING KOCHAB

The acclaimed poet Tony Crowley (who gave us the doggerel for remembering the Equation of Time) is also an enthusiast for barefoot navigation. He also invented the Polarum, a device designed for measuring the rotation of the northern circumpolar stars and from which the observer's longitude can be calculated. The Polarum is a work of art that incorporates prisms, light-emitting diodes and a spirit level. It is not something that you can improvise on a boat, but you might want to read about it in the back issues of *Practical Boat Owner*.[53]

However, Tony Crowley also has a method of obtaining a longitude from the circumpolar stars with little more than a UT watch and some arithmetic. This is based on the position of the bright star Kochab in relation to Polaris. Kochab is relatively easy to find; it is at the opposite end of Ursa Minor from the Pole Star (see Fig 3.12). Consequently, it rotates around Polaris once every 24 hours. To measure the angle Kochab makes in all its positions would be impossible without

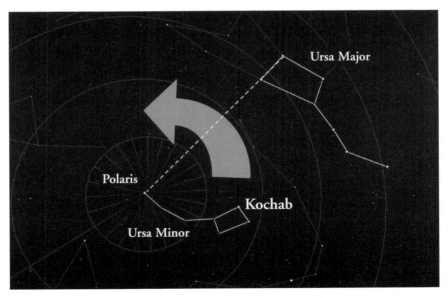

**Fig 3.12** The position of Kochab.

an instrument (hence the Polarum), but that is much less of a challenge when it is vertically above or below Polaris, or to the left or right of it by 90°.

This is a method that only really works in the northern hemisphere and you have to be far enough north if you are going to use Kochab when it is at 180° from the meridian, vertically below Polaris (see Fig 3.13).

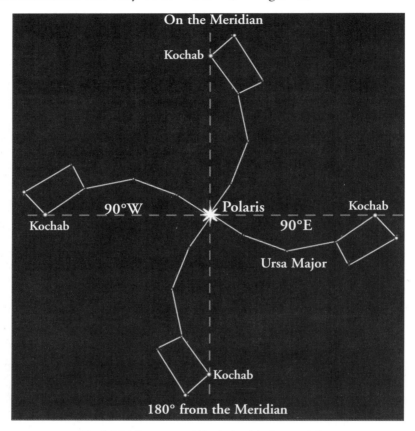

**Fig 3.13** Alignment of Kochab with the meridian.

To use the technique, the navigator has to obtain the UT time at which Kochab is in one of the four 'square' positions in relation to the Pole Star: vertically above, 90° east or west, or vertically below Polaris at 180°. Tony Crowley proposes a number of different ways in which these positions can be checked. A plumb line can be used for the vertical positions, or something with right-angled edges like a book. Place one edge along the horizon and try to align the other with the two stars. A carpenter's spirit level can be used to check the east and west positions. Being able to see the horizon obviously helps, especially if it is reasonably close to Ursa Minor; Crowley even proposes that with some experience it is possible to make a reasonable estimate of an alignment just by 'eye-balling' the stars.

Now here comes the calculation; when I described this method as a 'minimalist' approach to getting a longitude I was referring to the technology. The calculation is not particularly difficult, but there is a key piece of information that you need: the Greenwich Hour Angle of Aries. If you can't look this datum up in an almanac, you will have to do some additional arithmetic. First, though, you need to know what it is.

The position of a celestial object is determined by its declination (angle above the celestial horizon) and by how far its geographical position is around the globe from Greenwich (the equivalent of a longitude). This is called its 'Greenwich Hour Angle' (or GHA) and this changes according to the date and time. There are some 57 celestial objects that are used for navigation purposes; if GHA tables were included for each of these, then nautical almanacs would weigh more than your anchor. Because the distance between the stars doesn't change (well, not perceptibly), a different approach is employed. Almanacs include GHA tables for *Aries* so that at any one time you can look up its current position around the celestial sphere. This is measured from the exact point at which Aries rises above the celestial Equator. Don't spend too much time on deck looking out for this Aries – it doesn't exist any more. The original star used for this purpose drifted too far off target to do this job, and the starting gun now fires when a notional point in the blackness crosses the celestial Equator.

Now Aries has put a marker down, the position of all the other stars is given *in relation to the GHA of Aries*. You should be familiar with the nautical almanac but, if you are not, each page includes entries for each hour over three consecutive days. Aries is on the same page as the planets sun and moon, and is in the left-hand column. On the same page is a list of the stars used for navigation, each with its declination and something called the 'Sidereal Hour Angle' (SHA). The SHA is the angle it makes with Aries. If, therefore, we are going to calculate our longitude from Kochab, we need to know the GHA of Aries at the time we record that star passing the four cardinal points around Polaris. If you don't have an almanac to hand, you will have to work it out some other way and I'll return to that a little later.

Once we have the timing of Kochab and the GHA of Aries, the calculation is very straightforward. Here is Tony Crowley's method:

1  Write down the GHA of Aries at the time of the Kochab observation.
2  Add 137º 33.0 for the angular distance between Aries and Kochab. Kochab varies a little, but the average of 137º 19.2 is fine for our purposes. Tony Crowley recommends 137º 33.0 to remove a small discrepancy caused by the latitude of the observer.
3  Add or subtract 0º, 90º or 180º according to the position of Kochab in relation to Polaris (90º east is -90º, 90º west is +90º).
4  If the result is more than ±360º, subtract 360º.
5  The result of that is your longitude east of Greenwich (if negative) or west of Greenwich (if positive).

Table 3.7 gives a worked example. On 2 June 2007 a navigator times Kochab going through the 90°W position in relation to Polaris at 1001 GMT. What is his longitude?

| Longitude from Kochab | |
|---|---|
| GHA Aries at 1001 GMT | 40° 30.0 |
| Add SHA for Kochab | 40° 30.0<br>Kochab: 137° 33.0<br>GHA Kochab: 178° 03.0 |
| Which position? Add 90° | GHA Kochab: 178° 03.0<br>+ 90° 00.0<br>Longitude West: 268° 03.0 |
| Subtract from 360° for Longitude East | 360° 00.0<br>268° 03.0<br>**Longitude East: 091° 57.0** |

**Table 3.7**

Given the inherent inaccuracies with this interesting barefoot method, we can assume that our navigator's position is longitude 92° plus whatever latitude he got from Polaris while he was looking at that part of the sky.

Now we have to return to the problem of finding the GHA of Aries. If you have no access to an almanac and are unable even to call a friend, then it becomes necessary to calculate it from a known value. That known value needs to be a previous date and time at which Aries transited the Greenwich meridian. What follows are rough approximations, but they are better than nothing and they are easy to remember. On 21 September each year Aries transits Greenwich at the following *times*:

- 2255 in a leap year
- 2356 in the year after that
- 2357 in the year after that one and then
- 2358 in the last year before we have another leap year.

What you have to do next demands some care and patience and a prayer that you are making your observation of Kochab before the end of October:

1  For each day since the known transit, subtract four minutes and add four seconds.

2  For each hour between the transit at Greenwich and the time of the Kochab observation, multiply by 15.05º. Multiply each minute by 0.25º.

3  If the observation Kochab is before the time of Aries transit, subtract 360º. Otherwise, the result is the GHA of Aries.

Table 3.8 gives another worked example. Kochab was timed at 2358 on 6 October 2008, which is a leap year. What was the GHA of Aries at that time and date?

| Calculating the GHA of Aries | |
|---|---|
| Greenwich transfer of Aries on 21 September 2008 | 2355 |
| 6 October 2008 is 15 days later Subtract 15 x 4 minutes = -60 mins Add 15 x 4 secs = +60 secs | −60 mins + 1 min = −59 mins |
| Greenwich transit of Aries on 6 October 2008 | 2355 − 59 = 2256 |
| Difference between time of transit and time of Kochab observation | 2358 − 2256 = 1 hr 2 mins |
| Convert from time to angle 1 hour = 15.05º 2 mins = 2 x 0.25 = 0.50º | 15.05º + 0.50º = 15.55º |
| **GHA Aries at 2358 = 15.55º** (observation after transit) | **15.55º = 15º 33s** |

**Table 3.8**

There is another way of performing this calculation, but it involves multiplying and dividing numbers to three decimal places – not something you would really want to do in a liferaft. Now you have a value for GHA Aries, you can complete the calculation of a longitude from your GMT of Kochab.

## A COMBINED DECLINATION/EOT TABLE

The tables for the Declination of the Sun (Appendices 3 and 4) and the Equation of Time (Appendices 7 and 8) are the essentials needed by the barefoot navigator if he or she is to obtain a reasonable latitude and longitude. The two small tables replace that bulky nautical almanac! We save weight but, at the same time, sacrifice accuracy. Short of using a sextant, there is no way of improving the accuracy, so I decided to save even more space by combining the two tables. Both of them use the same dates (every four days throughout the year starting from 1 January), so I combined them into a single three-column table showing date, declination and EoT.

The combined table is shown in Appendix 13 and a colour version is available to download from my website. It is small enough to stick on the back of your DIY quadrant; if it isn't, your quadrant is not big enough! You have to experiment quite a lot to find a waterproof varnish that neither destroys the ink nor turns the paper into an impenetrable brown. I solved this problem when I bought a laminator. The laminated table can then be safely glued to the back of your quadrant.

# Plumbing the Depths

KNOWING THE DEPTH OF WATER under your keel is a major factor in lowering your personal stress level. Navigation without charts or with charts containing unreliable surveys of the bottom can benefit from an ability to plumb the depths. This is usually considered to be a pilotage issue, but I didn't include this under the heading 'Landfall' in Part 2 because we need a little more rudimentary technology.

Regular soundings showing a consistent decrease in depth implies an approach towards land. A sudden decrease followed by another increase might tell you that you've just crossed the bar. Being able to 'follow a contour' of identical soundings might help you to stand off a dangerous coastline at night. In fog, knowing the depth of water under your boat might be the only helpful piece of information you have.

The equipment needed has been well tested by our revered nautical forebears. The lead line or hand line has been defined as any line used to determine the depth of water a boat is passing over (usually just before it goes aground); traditionally this is a lead weight of 7lbs (a 'sounding lead', about 3kg) connected to a line marked off with ties every fathom:

> The proper way to mark a hand line is, black leather at 2 and 3 fathoms; white rag at 5; red rag at 7; white strip of leather, with a hole in it, at 10; and 13, 15 and 17 marked like 3, 5 and 7; two knots at 20; 3 at 30; and 4 at 40 with single pieces of cord at 25 and 35.
>
> R H Dana, 1855

A 'fathom', of course, is or was an obsolete measure of depth – 6ft or 1.83m. It originates from the Old English word for 'embrace', *faedm*, on the assumption that a man's outstretched arms extended to 6ft. But that is the least of our worries; all modern nautical charts have depths marked in metres. The real issue when we bob about on the ocean in our liferaft is: where are we going to find black leather, white rag, red rag and white leather? And where did I put that 3kg ingot of lead? Maybe we could cannibalise those horrible trainers?

In my grab-bag are two long lengths of 'para-cord', a very strong and versatile line. I also have a bundle of plastic cable-ties. The smallest of these will pull quite tightly onto the para-cord and are a practical way of marking off the depths; they are even colour-coded. You don't need to go to the same extent as Dana. The best advice is to work back from your main consideration: am I about to go aground? So the first mark needs to be, say, a metre below your keel. Remember to allow for the fact that you might be standing as you 'swing the lead' – or whatever it is that you have tied to the end of the line. The calculation might go like this: you draw 2m, but you are swinging from 2m above that. Now add 1m for safety and the first mark is positioned 5m above the lead. Now add some further marks at 5m intervals until you run out of cord or cable-ties.

The traditional technique with the line was to swing the lead ahead from the bow and to let it settle before hauling it back again; the preferred technique for a shirker was to just 'swing the lead' and make a guess, thus saving the effort of pulling the lead back. The trick is to throw it far enough ahead that the lead is on the bottom and the line is vertical and tight below you as you pass over it. Then check the mark.

I was leaving a marina once and the American diver on the next berth waved and shouted, 'May there always be a hand of water under your keel!' I was touched and shouted back, 'May there always be a lungful of air in your tank!'

# PART FOUR

# Survival Navigation

IF WHAT YOU LEARN from this book brings you pleasure and makes you a better navigator, then you will have made an old man very happy. If what you learn saves your life, then you will have made an old man dangerously ecstatic. But I must repeat the statement I made at the very beginning: please do the courses and please go to sea well-equipped. Sail safe. That's enough preaching; this final part of the book includes some important checklists…

# Emergency Kits and Grab-bags

THE TIME THAT BAREFOOT NAVIGATION really comes into play is when your life depends on it. But in the same situation, it is essential that you use the very best aids available, so let me reinforce that important distinction before we go any further.

If you consider Bowditch[54] to be definitive on these matters, this is what he says about survival navigation: 'The navigator should assemble a kit containing equipment for emergency navigation.' This list should contain:

## The Bowditch Survival Kit

1 *GPS.* At least one proven and personally tested handheld GPS receiver with waypoints and routes entered, and with plenty of spare batteries.
2 *A small, magnetic hand-bearing compass* such as is used in small craft navigation, to be used if all other compasses fail.
3 *A minimal set of paper charts* for the voyage at hand, ranging from small-scale to coastal to approach and perhaps harbor, for the most likely scenarios. A *pilot chart* for the ocean basin in question makes a good small-scale chart for offshore use.
4 *A notebook or journal* suitable for use as a deck log and for computations, plus maneuvering boards, graph paper, and position plotting sheets.
5 *Pencils, erasers, a straightedge, protractor or plotter, dividers and compasses, and a knife or pencil sharpener.*
6 *A timepiece.* The optimum timepiece is a quartz crystal chronometer, but any high-quality digital wristwatch will suffice if it is synchronized with the ship's chronometer. A portable radio capable of receiving time signals, together with a good wristwatch, will also suffice.
7 *A marine sextant.* (An inexpensive plastic sextant will suffice.) Several types are available commercially. The emergency sextant should be used periodically so its limitations and capabilities are fully understood.

8 *A celestial navigation calculator* and spare batteries, or a current *Nautical Almanac* and this book or a similar text. Another year's almanac can be used for stars and the sun without serious error by emergency standards. Some form of long-term almanac might be copied or pasted in the notebook.

9 *Tables.* Some form of table might be needed for reducing celestial observations if the celestial calculator fails. The *Nautical Almanac* produced by the US Naval Observatory contains detailed procedures for calculator sight reduction and a compact *sight reduction table.*

10 *Flashlight.* Check the batteries periodically and include extra batteries and bulbs in the kit.

11 *Portable radio.* A handheld VHF transceiver approved by the Federal Communications Commission for emergency use can establish communications with rescue authorities. A small portable radio may be used as a radio direction finder or for receiving time signals.

12 *An Emergency Position Indicating Radiobeacon (EPIRB)* and a *Search and Rescue Transponder (SART)* are absolutely essential.[54]

That seems fine to me, but kind of assumes that you are cruising on a battleship with an unlimited budget; I have sailed with skippers whose *main* navigation kit doesn't match this specification. A more practical approach might be to consider how little you can get away with. So what is the safe minimum?

All sea-going yachts, but especially those that make passage across oceans, should carry an emergency 'grab-bag' containing essential survival equipment. I consider a hand-held GPS with spare batteries, a hand-bearing compass and a pilot chart to fall into this category. Obviously there is a cost implication here, but each of these items will be available as back-up to whatever you are using on the vessel on a day-to-day basis and a plastic sextant would be better than nothing. The skipper will have primary responsibility for ensuring that the grab-bag makes it into the lifeboat or liferaft; but don't rely on him or her, they might be helping the crew over the side.

In addition to the boat's grab-bag, I believe that each member of the crew should have their own personal survival kit. Encouraging them to keep their passport and money in it will serve to ensure that they know where it is at any time. It will also serve to ensure that they take it with them when they have to abandon ship. Appendix 2 shows a checklist of what I keep in my personal kit. This is not the kind of kit that you will find packaged in a matchbox or tobacco tin; it is based primarily on the minimum that I'd want to be stranded with at sea or on land – and constrained by what will fit into a hiker's small utility bag. The bag used to go everywhere with me, usually stuffed into a backpack along with spare spectacles, whatever book I'm reading, and so forth. That is in the past tense because, since September 11 2001, trying to board any commercial air flight with a knife in your hand baggage is not a wonderful idea. So now it is packed into the sail bag that's going into the baggage hold.

Some of the items under the heading 'navigation' are worthy of comment. I know some navigators who relish taking the trouble to make a sketch map of the sea areas they will cover on each leg of their voyage. They usually do this on graph paper and claim that it enables them to get familiar with what's coming up. I'm usually too busy (or too lazy) for that and look out a chart with the appropriate scale, take it around to the marina office, and persuade them to photocopy it for me. In practice, I charm two copies from the office person, one for my personal survival kit, one for the grab-bag. Value can be added to these if you mark the directions of wind and current prevailing for the time of year.

One issue I haven't resolved is land maps. The solution here, I believe, is to make sketch maps of any island or remote coast that you might fetch up on; this is practical because *any* patch of land has more marks on it than even the biggest stretch of ocean. A copy of the noon sun table and the graph for the Equation of Time is in there permanently; I printed these from the computer in the smallest type I could read and then had them laminated.

The compass is the type that hikers use. Some hand-bearing compasses are too big to fit into the utility bag and, arguably, too expensive. The 'chronometer' is the medium-priced quartz watch set to Universal Time (GMT) that I described earlier. As you now know, a quadrant can be improvised from materials in the kit – the protractor, a length of fishing line, and something like the multi-tool or whistle as a plum bob.

Just as important as what is in the kit is what is in your head – information and attitude. Hopefully, this book has provided you with some basic information that will help when you are adrift at sea or stranded on a beach and there is no sign of an orange (or red-and-white) helicopter; that information needs to be in your head. But whatever you might have remembered, a positive attitude is the key to survival on land and sea.

Finally, some of you might ask what the use of navigation is if you have no control over your direction of movement. You are certainly better off in a boat than in a raft; all you can do on a raft is deploy the sea anchor. In a boat you can set a sail, and maybe even row or paddle once land is in sight. Being aware of where you are and what your options might be should work to reinforce that positive attitude.

# NOTES

1 Joshua Slocum, *Voyage of the 'Liberdade'*, originally published 1894. Published today by the Narrative Press, Inc, 2001, and also by other publishers.

2 For more information about the Royal Yachting Association, visit its website at www.rya.org.uk.

3 Tim Bartlett, *The RYA Book of Navigation*, Adlard Coles Nautical, London, 1996. 1998, 1999, 2000.

4 Pat Langley-Price and Philip Ouvry, *Ocean Yachtmaster*, Adlard Coles Nautical, London, 2002.

5 James Cook, *The Journals*, Penguin Classics, London 1999.

6 Thor Heyerdahl, *Kon-Tiki* (1948). In 1951, Heyerdahl won an Academy Award for his film of the voyage.

7 Brian M Fagan (Editor in Chief), *The Oxford Companion to Archaeology*, Oxford University Press, New York, Oxford, 1996.

8 Fagan, *The Oxford Companion to Archaeology*. Oxford University Press.

9 Peter Bellwood, *The Polynesians: Prehistory of an Island People*, Thames and Hudson, London, 1987 edn.

10 Jan Knappert, *Pacific Mythology*, Diamond Books, London, 1995 edn.

11 Sir Joseph Banks, *The Endeavour Journal*, 25 August 1768–12 July 1771. Entry for 21 July 1769.

12 Bellwood, *The Polynesians*.

13 I will not cite the source to save the author's blushes.

14 Bob Webb, *Comfort Zone Navigation*, http://www.motivation-tools.com/liki_tiki/polynesian_navigation.htm.

15 Webb, *Comfort Zone Navigation*, http://www.motivation-tools.com/liki_tiki/polynesian_navigation.htm.

16 Dava Sobel, *Longitude*, Fourth Estate, London, 1996.

17 *Voyage of the Odyssey*, a PBS documentary 17 August 2001: http://www.pbs.org/odyssey/odyssey/20010817_log_transcript.html. Quote from transcript.

18 Banks, *The Endeavour Journal*. Entry for 12 July 1769.

19 British Museum reference number Add. MS 21593.C.

20 Liesl Clark, *Ancient Navigation*, PBS website at: www.pbs.org/wgbh/nova/easter/civilization/navigation.html.

21 Quoted in *The Conquest and Occupation of Tahiti* by B G Corney, 1913–19. *Hakluyt Society*, vol 11, no 1, page 5.

22 Egil Skalla-Grimsson (Egil, son of Grim-the-Bald), *Egil's Saga*. Translated by Christine Fell, 1975.

23 André Dollinger, *An Introduction to the History and Culture of Pharaonic Egypt*. URL: http://nefertiti.iwebland.com/.

24 *Herodotus: The Histories 4.42*. Translated by Aubrey de Selincourt. It is thought that Herodotus lived between 480 and 420 BCE, so he was writing some 200 years after the events he described.

25 *Herodotus: The Histories 4.42*.

26 I-ching, *A Record of the Buddhist Religion*, vol II, folio 5a, Oxford 1896, English translation by J Takakusu.

27 Buzburg ibn Shahriyār, al-Ram-Hurmuzī, *Kitāb 'ajā'ib al-Hind*. Translated from Arabic by L M Devic, 1886. Quoted in George F Hourani, *Arab Seafaring*, Princeton University Press, New Jersey, 1979 edn.

28 *The Holy Koran* [6:97].

29 Hourani, *Arab Seafaring*.

30 R B Serjeant, *Hadramawt to Zanzibar: the pilot-poem of Nâkhûdhâ Sa'd Bâ Tâyi' of al-Hâmî*. Festschrift for James Kirkman, *Paideuma* 28:109–127, 1982. (Hadramawt is the mountainous region on Yemen's Gulf of Aden coast.)

31 Hourani, *Arab Seafaring*.

32 Jack Lagan, *A B Sea: A Loose-Footed Lexicon*, Seafarer Books, London, 2003.

33 Gavin Menzies, *1442: The Year China Discovered the World*, Bantam Press, London, 2002.

34 Robert Finlay, 'How Not to (Re)Write World History: Gavin Menzies and the Chinese Discovery of America', *Journal of World History*, vol 15, no 2, June 2004. This review paper is the ultimate antidote to Gavin Menzies's claims. It is available on the web at www.historycooperative.org/journals/jwh/15.2/finlay.html.

35 Science@NASA, *Total Lunar Eclipse*. URL: http://science.nasa.gov/headlines/y2004/13oct_lunareclipse.htm.

36 Sobel, *Longitude*.

37 Alan Gurney, *Compass: A Story of Innovation and Exploration*, Norton, New York and London, 2004.

38 Gurney, *Compass*.

39 Remember that the direction of a wind is described in terms of the direction from which it originates; for example a 'northerly wind' comes from the north.

40 Dennis Kawaharada, *Wayfinding, or Non-Instrument Navigation*, the Polynesian Navigation Society. URL: http://pvs.kcc.hawaii.edu/navigate/navigate.html.

41 Polynesian Navigation Society: Star Compasses. URL: http://pvs.kcc.hawaii.edu/navigate/stars.html. Keep in mind that the compasses shown are modern renditions of what was in the navigator's head.

42 Lagan, *A B Sea: A Loose-footed Lexicon*.

**43** 'Rare' because the photograph is a montage!

**44** Cook, *The Journals*.

**45** Francis Chichester, *The Lonely Sea and the Sky*, Hodder & Stoughton, London, 1964.

**46** Hourani, *Arab Seafaring*.

**47** David Lewis, *We, The Navigators*, University of Hawaii Press, Honolulu, 1972, 1994 (ISBN: 0-8248-1582-3).

**48** Mathew Wilson, *Bahamas Cruising Guide with the Turks and Caicos Islands*, Nomad Press, Florida. 4th edn, 2005. URL: www.bahamasguide.com.

**49** In practical terms, a vector is an arrow that represents a combination of speed and direction. These vectors can be a measurement of the speed and direction of wind and water and are used to modify the course you want to make good to provide a course to steer.

**50** Vladimir Peniakoff, *Popski's Private Army*, London, 2002, Cassell Military Paperbacks. (Originally published 1950.)

**51** Sobel, *Longitude*.

**52** Sobel, *Longitude*.

**53** Tony Crowley, 'What's a Polarum?' *Practical Boat Owner*, no 370, October 1997; and 'Pointer to the Stars', *Practical Boat Owner*, no 371, November 1997.

**54** Nathaniel Bowditch, LLD, *The American Practical Navigator*, 2002, © 2002, the National Imagery and Mapping Agency, US Government.

# RECOMMENDED FURTHER READING

## BOOKS

This is not intended as a comprehensive bibliography. The following books are recommended reading on aspects of barefoot navigation and the history of navigation. They were all in print at the time of writing.

Bowditch, Nathaniel, *The American Practical Navigator*, see entry for website.

Burch, David, *Emergency Navigation*, International Marine, Camden, Maine, 1986, 1990.

Cook, James, *The Journals*, Penguin Classics, London 1999.

Gurney, Alan, *Compass: A Story of Innovation and Exploration*, Norton, New York and London 2004.

Lewis, David, *We, the Navigators: The Ancient Art of Landfinding in the Pacific*, University of Hawaii Press, Honolulu 1972, 1994.

Schlereth, Hewitt, *Celestial Navigation in a Nutshell*, Sheridan House, New York, 2000. This is probably as simple as it gets.

## WEBSITES

These websites are a useful source of additional reading or as a source of research material. The URLs were good at the time of writing, but if any of them seem to be struck down by 'link rot', use a search engine to relocate them.

*Celestial Navigation*, Jim Thompson. This is a detailed and practical site devised and maintained by a Canadian sailor.
http://jimthompson.net/boating/Celestial_Navigation.htm.

*The American Practical Navigator*, Nathaniel Bowditch. This wonderfully detailed and definitive classic is published and maintained by the US National Imagery and Mapping Agency and is in the public domain. In my experience, the NIMA website is very slow but the whole of Bowditch is available in .pdf format here: www.irbs.com/bowditch/.

*William Falconer's Dictionary of the Marine*. This dictionary was originally published in London in 1780 under the full title of: *An Universal Dictionary Of The Marine: Or, A Copious Explanation Of The Technical Terms and Phrases Employed In The Construction, Equipment, Furniture, Machinery, Movements, And Military*

*Operations Of A Ship. Illustrated With variety of Original DESIGNS of SHIPPING, in different Situations; Together with separate VIEWS of their Masts, Sails, Yards, and Rigging. To which is annexed, A translation of the FRENCH Sea-Terms and Phrases, collected from the Works of Mess. DU HAMEL, AUBIN, SAVERIEN, &c.* The South Sea Project of James Cook University in Australia have turned this work into an interactive, searchable web site, a considerable task for which they must be commended! If you are interested in really old English and French nautical words pay the site a visit and have a browse. Fascinating stuff.
www.jcu.edu.au/aff/history/southseas/refs/falc/title.html

*The South Seas Project, James Cook University, Australia.* An excellent collection of primary source material mostly concerning the 18th century exploration of the South Pacific by the British. It includes meticulous transcriptions of the journals of Captain James Cook, Joseph Banks, John Hawkesworth, Samuel Wallis, Sidney Parkinson, James Morrison, and Henry Brook Adams.
http://www.jcu.edu.au/aff/history/southseas/

*A History of the International Date Line.* This is one huge illustrated web page containing everything you would want to know about the International Dateline. It was written by the Dutch astronomer Robert van Gent.
http://www.phys.uu.nl/~vgent/idl/idl.htm

*Columbus and Celestial Navigation.* Although Columbus was primarily a dead reckoning navigator, he did experiment with celestial navigation techniques from time to time. However, these experiments were usually unsuccessful – and in some cases, actually fraudulent. If Keith Pickering's introduction to this interesting page doesn't get your heart beating, nothing will. For more about Columbus – especially his likely landfall – start here: http://www1.minn.net/~keithp/ and then go on to http://www1.minn.net/~keithp/cn.htm

*The Astrolabe.* 'An instrument with a past and a future' it says at the top of the page. Start here to get yourself well-briefed on this venerable old navigation instrument. You can also buy a personalised astrolabe. http://astrolabes.org/

*Determination of Latitude by Francis Drake on the Coast of California in 1579.* This has a practical orientation for folks living in Northern California because you can make a field trip (by land or sea) to Bodega Harbor and other locations that are candidates for the site of Drake's landfall. Highly recommended – especially for children. http://www.longcamp.com/portus.html

*The History of Cartography, University of St Andrews, Scotland.* This first class review of chart-making is part of St Andrews University's excellent site on the history of mathematics.
www-history.mcs.st-and.ac.uk/HistTopics/Cartography.html

# Appendices

## APPENDIX 1: QUADRANT SCALE

*Note*: Ensure that the top edge of the scale is exactly parallel to the sighting edge of the board.

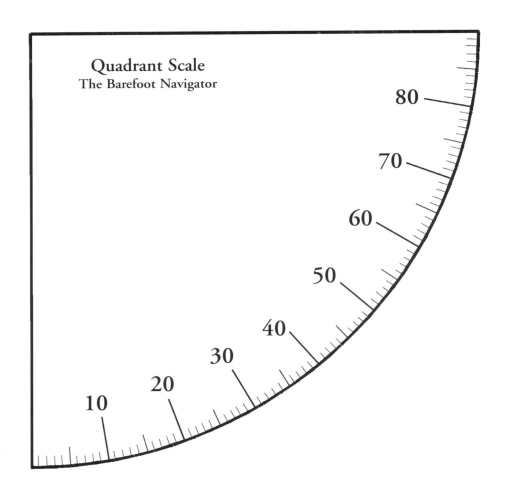

Quadrant Scale
**The Barefoot Navigator**

# APPENDIX 2: THE BAREFOOT NAVIGATOR'S SURVIVAL KIT

| Basic | | | |
|---|---|---|---|
| | Survival blanket | 1 | 'Space blanket' type |
| | Folding knife | 1 | Sturdy, stainless-steel blade |
| | Knife sharpener | 1 | Mine is a key fob |
| | Folding multi-tool | 1 | I have a key-fob Leatherman®, but a good Swiss Army Knife would be an alternative |
| | Para-cord | 10m | Much more if you have space |
| | Cable-ties | 10 | Variety of sizes and colours |
| | Signalling mirror | 1 | Heliograph |
| | Whistle | 1 | Mine is an Acme Thunderer® |
| | Small torch | 1 | Preferably waterproof: I use a MityLite® Submersible |
| | Spare batteries | 2 | For the torch |
| | Waterproof matches | 12 | With striking board |
| | Monofil fishing line | 20m | Can also be used to improvise animal traps on land |
| | Fishing hooks | 10 | Variety of sizes, all non-corrosive |
| | Sewing kit | 1 | Hotel freebie |
| | Waterproof wallet | 1 | For passport, cash etc |
| **First aid** | Adhesive plasters | | Waterproof |
| | Bandage | 1 | Roll |
| | Wound dressing | 1 | |
| | Aspirin | 12 | Caplets |
| | Antiseptic cream | 1 | Tube |
| | Sun block | 1 | Tube |
| | Water purification tablets | 10 | These do *not* desalinate of course. |
| **Navigation** | Compass | 1 | I have a small Suunto® |
| | Quartz watch | 1 | Set to UT (GMT) |
| | School protractor | 1 | For improvising a quadrant |

| | | | |
|---|---|---|---|
| | Plastic ruler | 1 | 15cm |
| | Chart/map of area | 1 | A photocopy or a sketch-map |
| | Pencil stubs | 2 | HB rather than 3B |
| | Equation of Time Graph | 1 | Reverse may be used for notes |
| | Noon Sun Table | 1 | Reverse may be used for notes |
| **Carrier** | Utility Bag | 1 | For the above: Mine is sold in trekking stores for hikers and is 15x10x5cm with sturdy belt clips and a shoulder strap. |

# APPENDIX 3: DECLINATION OF SUN FOR NOON AT GREENWICH

| January | | April | | July | | October | |
|---|---|---|---|---|---|---|---|
| 1 | −23.0 | 3 | 5.4 | 4 | 22.9 | 4 | −4.4 |
| 5 | −22.6 | 7 | 6.9 | 8 | 22.5 | 8 | −5.9 |
| 9 | −22.1 | 11 | 8.4 | 12 | 21.9 | 12 | −7.4 |
| 13 | −21.5 | 15 | 9.8 | 16 | 21.3 | 16 | −8.9 |
| 17 | −20.7 | 19 | 11.2 | 20 | 20.6 | 20 | −10.4 |
| 21 | −19.9 | 23 | 12.6 | 24 | 19.8 | 24 | −11.8 |
| 25 | −18.9 | 27 | 13.9 | 28 | 18.9 | 28 | −13.2 |
| 29 | −17.9 | | | | | | |
| **February** | | **May** | | **August** | | **November** | |
| 2 | −16.8 | 1 | 15.1 | 1 | 18.0 | 1 | −14.5 |
| 6 | −15.6 | 5 | 16.3 | 5 | 16.9 | 5 | −15.7 |
| 10 | −14.3 | 9 | 17.4 | 9 | 15.8 | 9 | −16.9 |
| 14 | −13.0 | 13 | 18.4 | 13 | 14.6 | 13 | −18.0 |
| 18 | −11.6 | 17 | 19.4 | 17 | 13.4 | 17 | −19.0 |
| 22 | −10.1 | 21 | 20.2 | 21 | 12.1 | 21 | −20.0 |
| 26 | −8.7 | 25 | 21.0 | 25 | 10.7 | 25 | −20.8 |
| | | 29 | 21.6 | 29 | 9.3 | 29 | −21.5 |
| **March** | | **June** | | **September** | | **December** | |
| 2 | −7.1 | 2 | 22.2 | 2 | 7.9 | 3 | −22.1 |
| 6 | −5.6 | 6 | 22.7 | 6 | 6.4 | 7 | −22.6 |
| 10 | −4.0 | 10 | 23.0 | 10 | 4.9 | 11 | −23.0 |
| 14 | −2.5 | 14 | 23.3 | 14 | 3.4 | 15 | −23.3 |
| 18 | −0.9 | 18 | 23.4 | 18 | 1.8 | 19 | −23.4 |
| 22 | 0.7 | 22 | 23.4 | 22 | 0.3 | 23 | −23.4 |
| 26 | 2.3 | 26 | 23.4 | 26 | −1.3 | 27 | −23.3 |
| 30 | 3.8 | 30 | 23.2 | 30 | −2.9 | 31 | −23.0 |

**The Barefoot Navigator: Declination of the Sun for 2006 and 2007**
**Updates at: jack-lagan.com**

*Note:* These declinations are good for 2006 and 2007.

Declinations are rounded to the nearest 0.1°.

This table can also be downloaded from the Barefoot Navigator website at: jack-lagan.com.

# APPENDIX 4: DECLINATION OF SUN (SMALL VERSION)

| January | | April | | July | | October | |
|---|---|---|---|---|---|---|---|
| 1 | −23.0 | 3 | 5.4 | 4 | 22.9 | 4 | −4.4 |
| 5 | −22.6 | 7 | 6.9 | 8 | 22.5 | 8 | −5.9 |
| 9 | −22.1 | 11 | 8.4 | 12 | 21.9 | 12 | −7.4 |
| 13 | −21.5 | 15 | 9.8 | 16 | 21.3 | 16 | −8.9 |
| 17 | −20.7 | 19 | 11.2 | 20 | 20.6 | 20 | −10.4 |
| 21 | −19.9 | 23 | 12.6 | 24 | 19.8 | 24 | −11.8 |
| 25 | −18.9 | 27 | 13.9 | 28 | 18.9 | 28 | −13.2 |
| 29 | −17.9 | | | | | | |

| February | | May | | August | | November | |
|---|---|---|---|---|---|---|---|
| 2 | −16.8 | 1 | 15.1 | 1 | 18.0 | 1 | −14.5 |
| 6 | −15.6 | 5 | 16.3 | 5 | 16.9 | 5 | −15.7 |
| 10 | −14.3 | 9 | 17.4 | 9 | 15.8 | 9 | −16.9 |
| 14 | −13.0 | 13 | 18.4 | 13 | 14.6 | 13 | −18.0 |
| 18 | −11.6 | 17 | 19.4 | 17 | 13.4 | 17 | −19.0 |
| 22 | −10.1 | 21 | 20.2 | 21 | 12.1 | 21 | −20.0 |
| 26 | −8.7 | 25 | 21.0 | 25 | 10.7 | 25 | −20.8 |
| | | 29 | 21.6 | 29 | 9.3 | 29 | −21.5 |

| March | | June | | September | | December | |
|---|---|---|---|---|---|---|---|
| 2 | −7.1 | 2 | 22.2 | 2 | 7.9 | 3 | −22.1 |
| 6 | −5.6 | 6 | 22.7 | 6 | 6.4 | 7 | −22.6 |
| 10 | −4.0 | 10 | 23.0 | 10 | 4.9 | 11 | −23.0 |
| 14 | −2.5 | 14 | 23.3 | 14 | 3.4 | 15 | −23.3 |
| 18 | −0.9 | 18 | 23.4 | 18 | 1.8 | 19 | −23.4 |
| 22 | 0.7 | 22 | 23.4 | 22 | 0.3 | 23 | −23.4 |
| 26 | 2.3 | 26 | 23.4 | 26 | −1.3 | 27 | −23.3 |
| 30 | 3.8 | 30 | 23.2 | 30 | −2.9 | 31 | −23.0 |

Four simple steps to estimate latitude (sun to south):

| | | |
|---|---|---|
| **1** | Use quadrant to read the altitude of the sun at local noon. | Example:<br>**alt = 35°** |
| **2** | Subtract altitude from 90° to obtain zenith distance. | ZD = 90° - alt<br>**ZD = 90° − 35° = 55°** |
| **3** | Use table above (or Appendix 4) to obtain the declination of the sun for date of sight. | Date = March 12<br>**Dec = −3.3°** |
| **4** | Add declination to zenith distance to obtain latitude. | Lat = ZD + Dec<br>**Lat = 55° − 3.3° = 51.7°** |

For calculation see also Table 3.3, page 102.

This table can also be downloaded from the Barefoot Navigator website at: www.jack-lagan.com.

# APPENDIX 5: SCHEMATIC FOR SUN-SHADOW BOARD

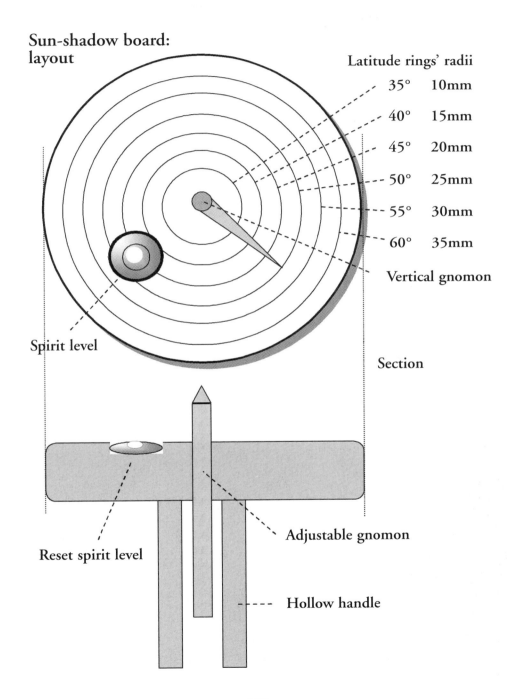

**Sun-shadow board: layout**

Latitude rings' radii

| | |
|---|---|
| 35° | 10mm |
| 40° | 15mm |
| 45° | 20mm |
| 50° | 25mm |
| 55° | 30mm |
| 60° | 35mm |

Vertical gnomon

Spirit level

Section

Reset spirit level

Adjustable gnomon

Hollow handle

# APPENDIX 6: GNOMON SETTINGS FOR THE SUN-SHADOW BOARD

| | 35 | 40 | 45 | 50 | 55 | 60 | | 35 | 40 | 45 | 50 | 55 | 60 |
|---|---|---|---|---|---|---|---|---|---|---|---|---|---|
| 1 Jan | 6 | 8 | 8 | 8 | 6 | 6 | 4 Jul | 47 | 49 | 49 | 49 | 48 | 46 |
| 5 Jan | 6 | 8 | 8 | 8 | 7 | 7 | 8 Jul | 45 | 48 | 48 | 48 | 47 | 46 |
| 9 Jan | 6 | 8 | 8 | 8 | 7 | 7 | 12 Jul | 43 | 46 | 47 | 47 | 46 | 45 |
| 13 Jan | 7 | 8 | 9 | 9 | 7 | 7 | 16 Jul | 41 | 45 | 46 | 46 | 45 | 44 |
| 17 Jan | 7 | 8 | 9 | 9 | 8 | 8 | 20 Jul | 39 | 43 | 44 | 45 | 44 | 43 |
| 21 Jan | 7 | 9 | 9 | 9 | 8 | 8 | 24 Jul | 37 | 41 | 43 | 43 | 43 | 42 |
| 25 Jan | 7 | 9 | 10 | 10 | 9 | 9 | 28 Jul | 35 | 39 | 41 | 42 | 41 | 40 |
| 29 Jan | 8 | 9 | 10 | 10 | 9 | 9 | | | | | | | |

| | 35 | 40 | 45 | 50 | 55 | 60 | | 35 | 40 | 45 | 50 | 55 | 60 |
|---|---|---|---|---|---|---|---|---|---|---|---|---|---|
| 2 Feb | 8 | 10 | 11 | 11 | 10 | 8 | 1 Aug | 33 | 37 | 39 | 40 | 40 | 39 |
| 6 Feb | 8 | 10 | 11 | 11 | 11 | 9 | 5 Aug | 31 | 35 | 38 | 38 | 38 | 38 |
| 10 Feb | 9 | 11 | 12 | 12 | 11 | 10 | 9 Aug | 29 | 34 | 36 | 37 | 37 | 36 |
| 14 Feb | 9 | 11 | 12 | 13 | 12 | 11 | 13 Aug | 27 | 32 | 34 | 35 | 35 | 35 |
| 18 Feb | 9 | 12 | 13 | 13 | 13 | 12 | 17 Aug | 25 | 30 | 33 | 34 | 34 | 33 |
| 22 Feb | 10 | 12 | 14 | 14 | 14 | 13 | 21 Aug | 24 | 28 | 31 | 32 | 32 | 32 |
| 26 Feb | 10 | 13 | 15 | 15 | 15 | 14 | 25 Aug | 22 | 27 | 29 | 31 | 31 | 30 |
| | | | | | | | 29 Aug | 21 | 25 | 28 | 29 | 29 | 29 |

| | 35 | 40 | 45 | 50 | 55 | 60 | | 35 | 40 | 45 | 50 | 55 | 60 |
|---|---|---|---|---|---|---|---|---|---|---|---|---|---|
| 2 Mar | 11 | 14 | 15 | 16 | 16 | 15 | 2 Sep | 20 | 24 | 27 | 28 | 28 | 27 |
| 6 Mar | 12 | 15 | 16 | 17 | 17 | 16 | 6 Sep | 18 | 23 | 25 | 26 | 27 | 26 |
| 10 Mar | 12 | 15 | 17 | 18 | 18 | 17 | 10 Sep | 17 | 21 | 24 | 25 | 25 | 25 |
| 14 Mar | 13 | 16 | 18 | 19 | 19 | 18 | 14 Sep | 16 | 20 | 23 | 24 | 24 | 23 |
| 18 Mar | 14 | 17 | 19 | 20 | 20 | 19 | 18 Sep | 15 | 19 | 21 | 22 | 23 | 22 |
| 22 Mar | 15 | 18 | 20 | 21 | 21 | 21 | 22 Sep | 14 | 18 | 20 | 21 | 21 | 21 |
| 26 Mar | 16 | 19 | 22 | 23 | 23 | 22 | 26 Sep | 14 | 17 | 19 | 20 | 20 | 19 |
| 30 Mar | 16 | 20 | 23 | 24 | 24 | 23 | 30 Sep | 13 | 16 | 18 | 19 | 19 | 18 |

| | 35 | 40 | 45 | 50 | 55 | 60 | | 35 | 40 | 45 | 50 | 55 | 60 |
|---|---|---|---|---|---|---|---|---|---|---|---|---|---|
| 3 Apr | 18 | 22 | 24 | 25 | 25 | 25 | 4 Oct | 12 | 15 | 17 | 18 | 18 | 17 |
| 7 Apr | 19 | 23 | 25 | 27 | 27 | 26 | 8 Oct | 12 | 15 | 16 | 17 | 17 | 16 |
| 11 Apr | 20 | 24 | 27 | 28 | 28 | 28 | 12 Oct | 11 | 14 | 15 | 16 | 16 | 15 |
| 15 Apr | 21 | 26 | 28 | 29 | 30 | 29 | 16 Oct | 10 | 13 | 15 | 15 | 15 | 14 |
| 19 Apr | 23 | 27 | 30 | 31 | 31 | 31 | 20 Oct | 10 | 12 | 14 | 14 | 14 | 13 |
| 23 Apr | 24 | 29 | 31 | 33 | 33 | 32 | 24 Oct | 9 | 12 | 13 | 13 | 13 | 12 |
| 27 Apr | 26 | 30 | 33 | 34 | 34 | 34 | 28 Oct | 9 | 11 | 12 | 13 | 12 | 11 |

| | 35 | 40 | 45 | 50 | 55 | 60 | | 35 | 40 | 45 | 50 | 55 | 60 |
|---|---|---|---|---|---|---|---|---|---|---|---|---|---|
| 1 May | 27 | 32 | 35 | 36 | 36 | 35 | 1 Nov | 9 | 11 | 12 | 12 | 11 | 10 |
| 5 May | 29 | 34 | 36 | 37 | 37 | 36 | 5 Nov | 8 | 10 | 11 | 11 | 11 | 9 |
| 9 May | 42 | 36 | 38 | 39 | 39 | 38 | 9 Nov | 8 | 10 | 11 | 11 | 10 | 8 |
| 13 May | 45 | 38 | 40 | 41 | 40 | 39 | 13 Nov | 8 | 9 | 10 | 10 | 9 | 8 |
| 17 May | 46 | 40 | 42 | 42 | 42 | 41 | 17 Nov | 7 | 9 | 10 | 10 | 9 | 7 |
| 21 May | 48 | 42 | 43 | 44 | 43 | 42 | 21 Nov | 7 | 9 | 9 | 9 | 8 | 6 |
| 25 May | 40 | 43 | 45 | 45 | 44 | 43 | 25 Nov | 7 | 8 | 9 | 9 | 8 | 6 |
| 29 May | 42 | 45 | 46 | 46 | 45 | 44 | 29 Nov | 7 | 8 | 9 | 8 | 7 | 5 |

| | 35 | 40 | 45 | 50 | 55 | 60 | | 35 | 40 | 45 | 50 | 55 | 60 |
|---|---|---|---|---|---|---|---|---|---|---|---|---|---|
| 2 Jun | 44 | 47 | 48 | 47 | 47 | 45 | 3 Dec | 6 | 8 | 8 | 8 | 7 | 5 |
| 6 Jun | 45 | 48 | 49 | 48 | 47 | 46 | 7 Dec | 6 | 8 | 8 | 8 | 7 | 5 |
| 10 Jun | 47 | 49 | 50 | 49 | 48 | 46 | 11 Dec | 6 | 8 | 8 | 8 | 6 | 4 |
| 14 Jun | 48 | 50 | 50 | 50 | 49 | 47 | 15 Dec | 6 | 8 | 8 | 8 | 6 | 4 |
| 18 Jun | 49 | 50 | 51 | 50 | 49 | 47 | 19 Dec | 6 | 8 | 8 | 7 | 6 | 4 |
| 22 Jun | 49 | 50 | 51 | 50 | 49 | 47 | 23 Dec | 6 | 8 | 8 | 7 | 6 | 4 |
| 26 Jun | 49 | 50 | 51 | 50 | 49 | 47 | 27 Dec | 6 | 8 | 8 | 8 | 6 | 4 |
| 30 Jun | 48 | 50 | 50 | 49 | 48 | 47 | 31 Dec | 6 | 8 | 8 | 8 | 6 | 4 |

For use with Sun-shadow board shown in Appendix 5.

# APPENDIX 7: GRAPH FOR THE EQUATION OF TIME (EoT)

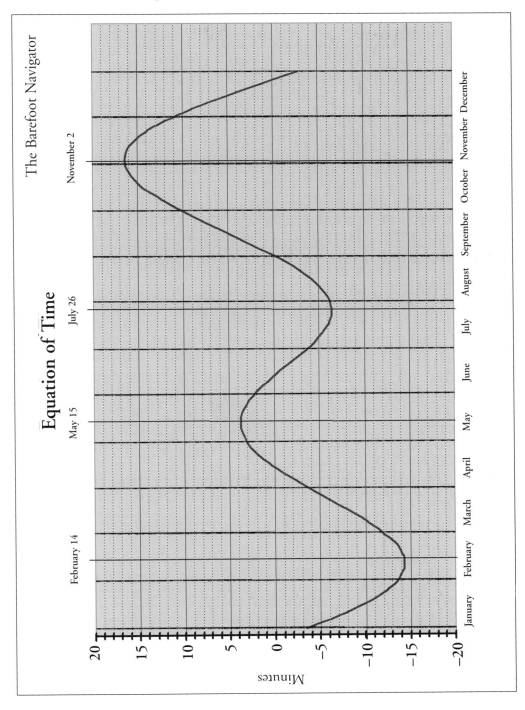

# APPENDIX 8: SMALL GRAPH FOR THE EQUATION OF TIME (EoT)

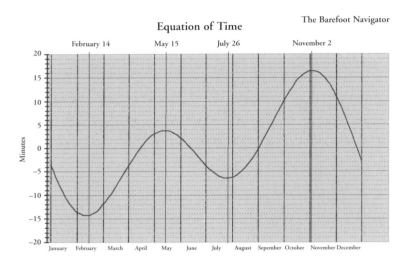

| The Equation of Time | | | | | | | |
|---|---|---|---|---|---|---|---|
| 1 Jan | −3.4 | 3 Apr | −3.5 | 4 Jul | −4.2 | 4 Oct | 11.1 |
| 5 | −5.2 | 7 | −2.4 | 8 | −4.8 | 8 | 12.3 |
| 9 | −7.0 | 11 | −1.2 | 12 | −5.4 | 12 | 13.3 |
| 13 | −8.6 | 15 | −0.2 | 16 | −5.9 | 16 | 14.3 |
| 17 | −10 | 19 | 0.7 | 20 | −6.2 | 20 | 15.1 |
| 21 | −11.2 | 23 | 1.6 | 24 | −6.4 | 24 | 15.7 |
| 25 | −12.3 | 27 | 2.3 | 28 | −6.4 | 28 | 16.1 |
| 29 | −13.1 | 1 May | 2.9 | 1 Aug | −6.3 | 1 Nov | 16.4 |
| 2 Feb | −13.7 | 5 | 3.3 | 5 | −6.0 | 5 | 16.4 |
| 6 | −14.1 | 9 | 3.6 | 9 | −5.5 | 9 | 16.2 |
| 10 | −14.3 | 13 | 3.7 | 13 | −4.9 | 13 | 15.8 |
| 14 | −14.3 | 17 | 3.7 | 17 | −4.1 | 17 | 15.1 |
| 18 | −14.1 | 21 | 3.6 | 21 | −3.2 | 21 | 14.2 |
| 22 | −13.7 | 25 | 3.2 | 25 | −2.2 | 25 | 13.2 |
| 26 | −13.1 | 29 | 2.8 | 29 | −1.1 | 29 | 11.9 |
| 2 Mar | −12.2 | 2 Jun | 2.2 | 2 Sep | 0.1 | 3 Dec | 10.4 |
| 6 | −11.5 | 6 | 1.6 | 6 | 1.5 | 7 | 8.8 |
| 10 | −10.5 | 10 | 0.8 | 10 | 2.8 | 11 | 7.0 |
| 14 | −9.5 | 14 | 0 | 14 | 4.2 | 15 | 5.1 |
| 18 | −8.3 | 18 | −0.8 | 18 | 5.6 | 19 | 3.2 |
| 22 | −7.1 | 22 | −1.7 | 22 | 7.0 | 23 | 1.2 |
| 26 | −5.9 | 26 | −2.6 | 26 | 8.4 | 27 | −0.8 |
| 30 | −4.7 | 30 | −3.4 | 30 | 9.8 | 31 | −2.8 |
| The Barefoot Navigator (EoT in minutes) | | | | | | | |

# APPENDIX 9: THE BEAUFORT SCALE

Originally devised in 1806 by Rear Admiral Sir Francis Beaufort (when he was a mere Commander), this table became internationally recognised in 1874 and was most recently upgraded in 1926.

| Force | Wind speed (knots) | Description | Sea state | Wave height (m) |
|---|---|---|---|---|
| 0 | 0–1 | Calm | Like a mill-pond | 0 |
| 1 | 1–3 | Light air | Ripples | 0 |
| 2 | 4–6 | Light breeze | Smooth, small wavelets | 0.1 |
| 3 | 7–10 | Gentle breeze | Large wavelets | 0.4 |
| 4 | 11–16 | Moderate breeze | Small waves, fairly frequent white caps | 1 |
| 5 | 17–21 | Fresh breeze | Moderate waves, many white caps, some spray | 2 |
| 6 | 22–27 | Strong breeze | Large waves, white foam crests, more spray | 3 |
| 7 | 28–33 | Near gale | Sea heaps up, white foam streaks from crests | 4 |
| 8 | 34–40 | Gale | Moderately high waves of greater length, spindrift with foamy streaks | 5.5 |
| 9 | 41–47 | Severe gale | High waves with tumbling crests, dense foam and spray affecting visibility | 7 |
| 10 | 48–55 | Storm | Very high waves with long overhanging crests, heavy tumbling sea | 9 |
| 11 | 56–63 | Violent storm | Exceptionally high waves, sea covered with long white patches of foam | 11 |
| 12 | 64 plus | Hurricane | Air filled with foam and spray, sea white with driving spray, visibility seriously affected | 14 |

# APPENDIX 10: GLOBAL POSITION
# EMERGENCY LOCATOR

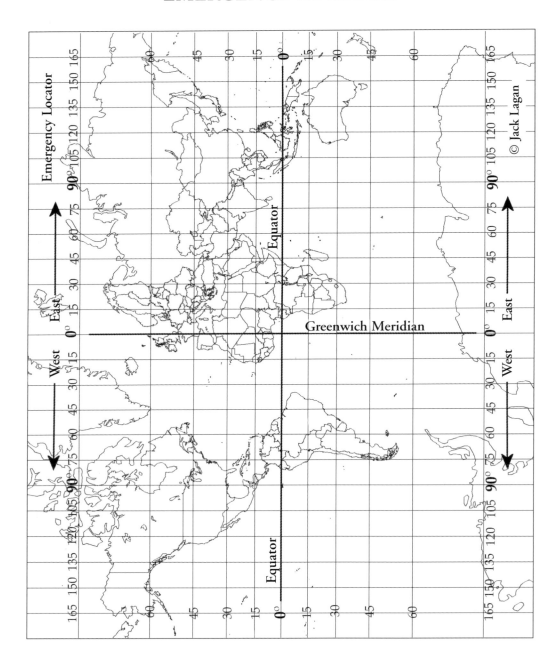

# APPENDIX 11: STANDARD TIME ZONES

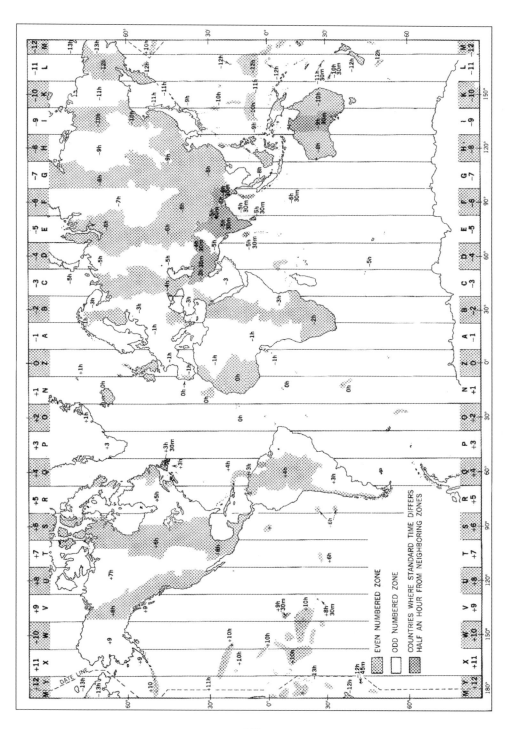

# APPENDIX 12: WORLD OCEAN CURRENTS

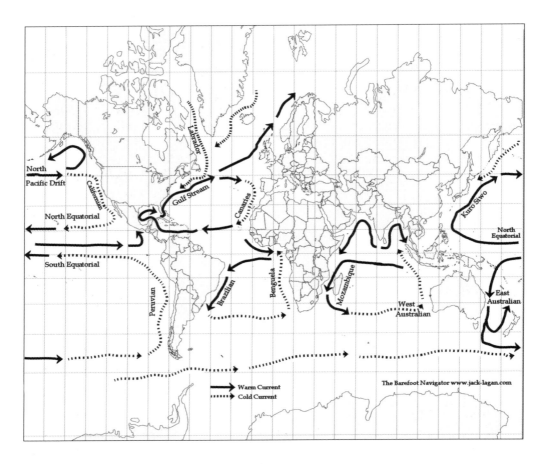

# APPENDIX 13: COMBINED TABLE FOR DECLINATION AND EQUATION OF TIME (EoT)

## Declination of Sun and the Equation of Time

| | Dec | EoT | | Dec | EoT | | Dec | EoT | | Dec | EoT |
|---|---|---|---|---|---|---|---|---|---|---|---|
| **January** | | | **April** | | | **July** | | | **October** | | |
| 1 | −23.0 | −3.4 | 3 | 5.4 | −3.5 | 4 | 22.9 | −4.2 | 4 | −4.4 | 11.1 |
| 5 | −22.6 | −5.2 | 7 | 6.9 | −2.4 | 8 | 22.5 | −4.8 | 8 | −5.9 | 12.3 |
| 9 | −22.1 | −7.0 | 11 | 8.4 | −1.2 | 12 | 21.9 | −5.4 | 12 | −7.4 | 13.3 |
| 13 | −21.5 | −8.6 | 15 | 9.8 | −0.2 | 16 | 21.3 | −5.9 | 16 | −8.9 | 14.3 |
| 17 | −20.7 | −10 | 19 | 11.2 | 0.7 | 20 | 20.6 | −6.2 | 20 | −10.4 | 15.1 |
| 21 | −19.9 | −11.2 | 23 | 12.6 | 1.6 | 24 | 19.8 | −6.4 | 24 | −11.8 | 15.7 |
| 25 | −18.9 | −12.3 | 27 | 13.9 | 2.3 | 28 | 18.9 | −6.4 | 28 | −13.2 | 16.1 |
| 29 | −17.9 | −13.1 | | | | | | | | | |
| **February** | | | **May** | | | **August** | | | **November** | | |
| 2 | −16.8 | −13.7 | 1 | 15.1 | 2.9 | 1 | 18.0 | −6.3 | 1 | −14.5 | 16.4 |
| 6 | −15.6 | −14.1 | 5 | 16.3 | 3.3 | 5 | 16.9 | −6.0 | 5 | −15.7 | 16.4 |
| 10 | −14.3 | −14.3 | 9 | 17.4 | 3.6 | 9 | 15.8 | −5.5 | 9 | −16.9 | 16.2 |
| 14 | −13.0 | −14.3 | 13 | 18.4 | 3.7 | 13 | 14.6 | −4.9 | 13 | −18.0 | 15.8 |
| 18 | −11.6 | −14.1 | 17 | 19.4 | 3.7 | 17 | 13.4 | −4.1 | 17 | −19.0 | 15.1 |
| 22 | −10.1 | −13.7 | 21 | 20.2 | 3.6 | 21 | 12.1 | −3.2 | 21 | −20.0 | 14.2 |
| 26 | −8.7 | −13.1 | 25 | 21.0 | 3.2 | 25 | 10.7 | −2.2 | 25 | −20.8 | 13.2 |
| | | | 29 | 21.6 | 2.8 | 29 | 9.3 | −1.1 | 29 | −21.5 | 11.9 |
| **March** | | | **June** | | | **September** | | | **December** | | |
| 2 | −7.1 | −12.2 | 2 | 22.2 | 2.2 | 2 | 7.9 | 0.1 | 3 | −22.1 | 10.4 |
| 6 | −5.6 | −11.5 | 6 | 22.7 | 1.6 | 6 | 6.4 | 1.5 | 7 | −22.6 | 8.8 |
| 10 | −4.0 | −10.5 | 10 | 23.0 | 0.8 | 10 | 4.9 | 2.8 | 11 | −23.0 | 7.0 |
| 14 | −2.5 | −9.5 | 14 | 23.3 | 0 | 14 | 3.4 | 4.2 | 15 | −23.3 | 5.1 |
| 18 | −0.9 | −8.3 | 18 | 23.4 | −0.8 | 18 | 1.8 | 5.6 | 19 | −23.4 | 3.2 |
| 22 | 0.7 | −7.1 | 22 | 23.4 | −1.7 | 22 | 0.3 | 7.0 | 23 | −23.4 | 1.2 |
| 26 | 2.3 | −5.9 | 26 | 23.4 | −2.6 | 26 | −1.3 | 8.4 | 27 | −23.3 | −0.8 |
| 30 | 3.8 | −4.7 | 30 | 23.2 | −3.4 | 30 | −2.9 | 9.8 | 31 | −23.0 | −2.8 |

Declination for 2006, 2007 © Jack Lagan

A colour version of this table can be downloaded from the Barefoot Navigator website at: www.jack-lagan.com.

# Index